AF512311

# The Muse with Wings

Air Marshal **VK Verma** AVSM, VM, VSM

KNOWLEDGE WORLD

KW Publishers Pvt Ltd

New Delhi

KNOWLEDGE WORLD

A KW Publishers Book
www.kwpublishers.com

© 2008, Air Marshal VK Verma

All rights reserved. No part of this publication may be reproduced, stored in a retrieval system, or transmitted in any form or by any means, electronic, mechanical, photocopying, recording or otherwise, without the prior written permission of the copyright owner.

ISBN 10: 81-87966-94-7
ISBN 13: 978-81-87966-94-4

Published in India by

Kalpana Shukla
KW Publishers Pvt Ltd
4676/21, First Floor, Ansari Road, Daryaganj, New Delhi 110002
email: knowledgeworld@vsnl.net / online.kw@gmail.com

Typeset by Black Innovation, New Delhi and Printed at Rajkamal Electric Press, New Delhi
Illustrations by Corporal A Dayal Pred, Institute of Flight Safety, New Delhi

***Dedicated to***

*My wife Sangita, who stood by me through the tumultuous times, kept me grounded and gave me the strength to "keep flying".*

# Contents

Foreword by Chief of the Air Staff vii

SECTION – I: The Winged Warrior

The Muse with Wings 3

GESTALT 6

One Track Mind 9

A Little Foreplay 13

Romance of the Night 16

Situational Awareness 21

The Dreamer 24

Address to Cadets 28

Flight Safety and Operational Effectiveness 31

SECTION – II: Operations

Decibels at a Fighter Base 37

The Robot in You 40

But I Believe it is Permitted 44

The Captain's Predicament 46

From the Files 49

Standard Operating Procedures (SOPs) 53

SECTION – III: Flight Safety: Qualitative Analysis

Flight Safety Statistics in Perspective 59

Flying Programme 61

KBC of Flight Safety 65
Bird Strikes 69
Towards a Better Work Ethos 76
Interpersonal Relationship 79
Annual Medical Examination Versus the Winged Warrior 81
Quality Output from Op Inspectors 86
New Year Resolution 96
Quality Audit 97

**SECTION IV: Beyond Flight: The Cyber Space**

Disinformation and Media Management 105
Indigenisation Vs Import: Indian Defence Industry 118
Jointness: The British Model 122

एयर चीफ मार्शल एफ एच मेजर
प वि से मे अ वि से मे शौ च वा मे ए डी सी
Air Chief Marshal F H Major
PVSM AVSM SC VM ADC
Tel : (011) Off : 23012517
Res : 23017300
Fax : 23018853
E-mail : airhouse@bol.net.in

वायु सेना मुख्यालय
नई दिल्ली-110 011
Air Headquarters
New Delhi- 110 011

# FOREWORD

The uniqueness of military aviation stands out distinctly. It is driven by mission-accomplishment, is extremely expensive and each loss is exorbitantly difficult to accept. Each accident that we sustain has long-term ramifications. It not only erodes our mission accomplishment and operational capability but also entails an irreplaceable loss in human resource as well. Therefore, every Air Warrior needs to understand very clearly that flight safety and operational effectiveness cannot be segregated into two individual entities. They complement each other. Operational capability depends on good training and this should also include all facets of flight safety. Importance of good communication, crew resource management, relevance of human factors, cognition and situational awareness are as relevant as exercise briefings.

It is, therefore, a pleasure when someone as experienced and with the right background puts all these issues in perspective in an easy to read format.

The articles are a lifetime collection of experiences and lessons learnt, with remedial measures. A must read by any pilot, who aspires to improve himself and his environment. I would exhort him to keep his pen flowing and continue to contribute towards enhancement of Flight Safety.

Jai Hind

AIR CHIEF MARSHAL
CHIEF OF THE AIR STAFF

09 Jun 08

**SECTION – I**

# THE WINGED WARRIOR

# The Muse With Wings

The typical image of a military aviator is a self-opinionated, cocksure, brow-beating braggart who refuses to keep his feet on mother earth, is forever walking a few inches above it and wears the demeanour of an immortal whom even God can't touch. Down to earth, humble, simple are adjectives that are not expected to sit easily on the image of this genre. But the military profession demands a disciplined and dedicated aviator who delivers the punch accurately when called upon to do so. How does one reconcile these contradictions?

Actually, there is no contradiction. Both represent two facets of the same image. Underneath each loud-mouthed brow-beating braggart sits a professional waiting for his turn or may be the other way around.

But the community, famous for outbursts and opinions, is eerily silent. The editor keeps asking me to send in more articles as his stock is generally low. This is where you come in. It is not possible that you are not worked up or passionate about some issue or the other. What is it that keeps you silent? There are two factors at work here. One is fear that keeps us from voicing our opinions whenever we suspect an issue to be controversial. We are worried that we may make fools of ourselves. From childhood, we are trained to be agreeable and we learn not to upset this state. Are military aviators so subdued! I hope not. Whither the self-opinionated braggart!

The second factor that keeps us silent is that our views may not be liked or may be labelled as irrational, not worthy, not acceptable, etc. In short, we would not like to express our thoughts for fear that they may not be politically correct. But if all of us shun controversy and stay within the safe bounds of acceptability, there would never be any growth and improvement and the Air Force would stagnate and disintegrate a la the Soviet Empire!

The foundation of any flight safety programme is communication. Share your experience and let others learn from your mistakes or how you learnt from them. The business of aviation is now a century old, and like history, we keep repeating our mistakes. There is a wealth of experience lying untapped amongst you all in the form of anecdotes, stories, mishaps averted, near miss, etc. Let it all flow out of the four walls of a crew room or a bar, and appear in print.

When you begin to write, you will discover that the written word has a power of its own. Let me repeat what an Air Marshal once quoted to me at the bar years ago when one evening I was busy sorting out the ills of the Air Force socially in the traditional aircrew fashion. He said,

"Silence makes a wise man;
Conference makes a ready man;
And only Writing makes a complete man.
I want a service paper on the subject within a fortnight."

So I sat down to pen my controversial opinion and what did I discover! That once the written words faced me, somehow the fizz of the controversy disappeared and the answers appeared within my reach. The written word forces one to consider so many more pros and cons than the spoken word. It helps in demisting the thought process and allows clarity to descend. It is not for nothing that the purists believe in the importance of the course at Wellington. So, may be, when you put your thoughts on paper, you may end up refining them and give them the necessary sheen of logic or may be the attempt will make you discard your long held views and look around for another vantage point.

So will you get your pen to paper and help elevate the flight safety programme by contributing your opinion/experience to this magazine? Perhaps, you are innovative in your approach and may be the whole Air Force may benefit from it. May be the lessons learnt by you are actually contagious and can prevent accidents. Perhaps your pen can cause a few stuck up faces to release their muscles and allow what may be approximately termed as a 'smile' to appear. May be you are the funny bone tickler. So arise the author in our military aviator and zoom up on the pages of our Journal. May "The Muse" provide you the power of its wings.❑

# GESTALT

- **Gestalt:** An organised whole that is perceived as more than the sum of its parts.
- **Gestalt Psychology:** A movement in psychology seeking to explain perceptions as gestalts rather than analysing their constituents.

Why am I introducing this quaint, German sounding word in a magazine that is an easy reading delight for the aviation community? Because I want to disturb the gestalt.

Let me explain. Picture an early morning scene on an airfield. Lots of fighter aircraft parked on the tarmac, looking so docile and peaceful, what with canopy covers and intake blankings in place. The sun struggling to break onto the horizon. Suddenly, the morning shift arrives and the gestalt changes. Appas or starting aggregates cough up, bowsers top up the aircraft, lots of technicians move about checking various parts and systems of the aircraft to ascertain its fitness to fly. An hour later, the scene changes. Aircraft are now ready, starting aggregates connected, technicians are congregating near the DSS desk, waiting for the pilots to arrive. The decibels on the tarmac have descended to a low, as if there is a lull before the storm. The scene actually is full of tranquillity, yet the spring is just waiting to uncoil. Sometimes this tranquillity gives way to boredom, when the pilots are delayed due to unexpected reasons like non-availability of a diversion or unserviceablity of a RANAD at base. Generally, such delays and their reasons take time to arrive at the desk, so the mood remains positive but passive.

As the pilots start arriving, the scene changes again. The technicians leave the desk area and head for the aircraft. Decibels on the tarmac commence their upward climb matching the pilot's entry into the cockpit and the mean machines rev up a crescendo of machismo, moving out of

---

- Concise Oxford Dictionary

the flight line threateningly. Beware of the air warrior on his way to touch the sky with glory!

I just described a few scenes on the flight line. Each scene has its own gestalt. Introduce anything unusual in the scene, it will disturb the harmony or change the gestalt. Picture the initial scenes. A bowser breaks down on its way out after topping up an aircraft. It will disturb the gestalt. Move to the next scene where technicians are awaiting the pilots, bring in the CEO instead, in his Gypsy, on the tarmac at this time and the whole gestalt will change. Similarly, in the scene where the aircraft are starting up and moving out of the flight line, any aircraft suddenly switching off would alter the gestalt. In our own way, each of us is familiar with the 'gestalt' on the flight line as we encounter these scenes regularly on each flying day.

How do we approach the flight line? Each of us has his own way of approaching the flight line. Some approach it in a highly focussed manner – move purposefully to the desk, sign on the F.700 and get to the aircraft. Some move in a mechanical way with their mind elsewhere – probably sorting out the complexities of the sortie on their way to the cockpit. Some have a casual, easygoing approach. Yet others use their extrovert nature to bond with the men befriending one and all on the way to the cockpit. Many formation leaders continue to give instructions/tips to their team members till they reach the parking slots. Some flight commanders use this as an opportunity to interact with the engineers and clarify the day's plan. The variety is enormous. Is there anything wrong in this? Well, yes and no, when Lady Luck has you on her wings – all these approaches are right. The day she chooses to shift house – most of these approaches have the potential to become the weak link in the chain of accidents/incidents.

The safety halo always sits on the head that does quality work. Any absentmindedness, non-adherence to standard operating procedures (SOPs), unfocussed activity, and the safety halo will evaporate and not be seen around you. So, how do you retain the safety halo?

The briefing for the sortie must finish in the briefing room. There must be some time available post-briefing where your mind unravels the various inputs it has received, sorts them out and then sort of stitches them up. The F 700 at the desk must get full attention so that you are ready to pick out any aberration/advice/noting available there. As you approach the dispersal, slow down, and absorb the scene unfolding in front. Get the gestalt. Where is the sun? Which way is the wind blowing? What is the cloud state? Is there anything unusual happening on the tarmac? Absorb the scene and let your subconscious tackle the oddities. Whether you realise it or not, your subconscious computer continuously updates its data bank. It will straightaway notice that for the planned four aircraft startup, the gang size is too small, vice versa or just the right size. Does your allotted aircraft have the fire extinguisher? Is starting aggregate positioned / connected?

Now, as you get closer, focus on aircraft covers, its top and bottom surfaces and all panels. Is there anything hanging loose? Are all the covers in place? Some of them will need to be removed while a few will get removed later in the sequence. Do all panels appear closed? A little distance short of the aircraft, in a few focussed glances, you will get all this information. For those of you who have not approached the tarmac in this manner, initially it will require a conscious effort to glean all these bits. With practice, it will become a habit and then your second nature.

Now you are ready for your external checks. Most of us go from point to point, check to check. Do that, but add another routine in this scheme. As you complete the checks in the zone of front fuselage, step back and check the full front fuselage and look for oddities/observations. Do this with the undersurface and the top of the wings. The same goes for rear fuselage. After you have checked the tail parachute panel and the jet nozzle area, step back a few paces and look at the full rear view of the aircraft. Repeat these steps on the other half of the aircraft. With the external checks completed, you are now ready for entry into the cockpit.

You will not see it around your head. But if you follow the methodology given above each time, then, as you put the helmet on, the safety halo will quickly form around your head.

Enjoy the sortie. ❑

# One Track Mind

One track mind is a term associated generally with a few of our ilk who can only think and talk sex. Even when you seriously describe your debacle on the golf course, they would be busy visualising antics of the bedroom variety. Their one track mind will not allow them any other version of the 'hole'.The smirk on their face would confirm the colour of the film their mind is seeing. Let me acquaint you with another single track of our mind which all of us possess – the decision-making track. It is commonly believed that man is gifted and has the ability to do many things simultaneously. Don't we listen to music and study at the same time? Don't we drive and talk? Of course, we do. However, when it comes to decision-making, we all possess only a single track. It is essential that all of us, specially the pilots, understand this.

Learning the basic flying skills initially requires a lot of conscious thought and decision-making. However, practising the basic skills allows you to learn the responses that are needed for manipulating the aircraft. Slowly, all this is translated into motor skills, which then do not require much conscious thought.

Please note that I have used the words 'basic flying skill' and 'much conscious thought' in the paragraph above. This is because flying is much more than just basic motor skill and it requires a lot of conscious thought and a helluva lot of decision-making. In fact, someone has defined piloting as a summation of motor skills and decision-making.

Now let us focus on the decision-making. The concept of the single decision channel is well established, yet, many people's first reaction to this idea is to protest that they can do two things simultaneously. On the face of it, they are right. Closer examination reveals that they are, in fact, simply scanning from one source of information to another very rapidly. A very common example cited is of driving and talking simultaneously. Watch the same person suddenly becoming quiet when traffic density increases or while overtaking, he finds an approaching vehicle in his path. He has given up scanning and is concentrating on only one source of information.

Lab tests have shown that when different messages are put into the right and left ears, the listener attends to only one side and will not be able to tell about the message in the other ear. It does not matter whether the other message comes to the ear, eye or to the seat of the pants, that area popularly renowned as the location of a mysterious 'instinctive' knowledge. Man, in fact, can only attend to one thing at a time. It is his central decision-making channel that limits the speed at which he can process the information. The very purpose of a horn, a master blinker or a Natasha is to attract your attention and couple it with an override for your decision channel. Yet, we are all familiar with any number of instances when warning signals are ignored by aircrew. Deliberations in courts of enquiries are filled with "Preoccupied with an emergency....... Pilot did not monitor the R/T call," etc.

During flying, an enormous amount of stimuli is perceived by the pilot in the form of visual images, sounds, smell, taste and feel. These are all picked up by the sense organs and the receptors in our ears and also by the famous rear end, which a lot of pilots claim to be using for flying. All these are filtered in our brain, which then connects and converts them into meaningful and relevant info bytes. These info bytes are then processed by the decision-making channel and the output in the form of relevant action / inaction is produced. It is worth noting that while one info byte is being processed by the decision channel, other items, which arrive at the same time, must await their turn in a memory store because the decision channel can handle items only sequentially – one at a time.

We have two memory stores – one a short-term memory store and another a long-term memory store. It is known that items waiting in the short-term memory store are quite likely to be forgotten very quickly. Suppose you are told by ATC to descend to a particular level. Simultaneously, information is given to you by radar of the proximity of another aircraft. Chances are that by the time you deal with this threat of collision, you are likely to forget the level you were cleared to descend to. The short-term memory is capable of holding only a few items for a brief period. Typically, seven items for 15 seconds, before they are forgotten. It is, in fact, notorious for forgetting. A message from ATC to change frequency to a specified frequency will remain in your memory long enough for you to select the frequency. Any delay or any excess of additional information and you will probably select the wrong frequency. That is why RT sets have preset frequencies – so that you don't have to recall 118.8, etc. This "seven items for 15 seconds" varies from person to person and also varies for the same person under different levels of stress.

The long-term memory is where information is filed away for later use. The information may need to be retrieved several minutes, hours, or days later. Sometimes, even years later. At times, there may be problems and delays in retrieving the information, especially if it has not been recalled or used for some time.

In a decision cycle, the stimulus is received, processed and the decision made. This is then followed by action and feedback. Action will be initiated by a conscious decision from the brain or by a motor programme that is running. A series of electrical signals will be sent along the motor nerves to the appropriate muscles for the action to commence. It could be speech, body movement, or a decision not to act. The results will be perceived by the mind-body combination and if the results indicate further action is needed, it will be produced. For example, imagine yourself rolling out on finals. In case you are not aligned properly with the runway, you will automatically produce the control inputs that will result in an alignment. This may happen consciously if you are inexperienced or automatically through a motor programme run by your robot if you are experienced.

The single track decision-maker is adequate to handle situations that arise in a normal sortie. Its limited capacity is exposed when complex situations arise in which, even though all the parts are working well, there is still so much information that the channel becomes overloaded. The response to an overload will depend upon individuals. Some will deal with each info byte quickly but badly. Some may concentrate on one source and exclude all else. Some tend to ignore all inputs. Some confuse information obtained from two or more sources. A few ignore all inputs and seek refuge in a totally irrelevant activity. On the ground, overload of this kind may not be disastrous as one can delay decisions or seek yet more information. In the air, such a luxury is absent and time is in short supply. This time compression can further impose its penalties by forcing one to make the wrong choices.

So now you know about your single track decision-making channel. What good will all this analysis and knowledge do? Well, it will help you identify the weak links in the chain. One weak link which can be strengthened is your memory store. Periodically recalling important information from memory enables it to be recalled more readily when you need it. For this reason, a daily emergency session in the briefing room is a good thing and must be continued and insisted upon. New material being learnt must be given full attention. If you understand it thoroughly and organise the various info bytes logically into your brain, retrieval is easier. Chunking information bits together and mnemonics like CTAFFIOP are some methods to improve memory. Learning *in situ* e.g. learning checks, procedures and emergencies in an actual cockpit or a simulator helps both in storing the information better and retrieval when needed.

The next link to improve is your aviation related knowledge levels. Any time one is faced with a new info byte, the mind searches its long-term memory store for a connection that can help it handle the info byte properly. If your knowledge levels are high, the faster will be the decision channel in handling the info byte. This will ensure that your processing speed is fast. You must aim to be like the Pentium 4s rather that the 286, 386 or 486 variety. Once your processing speed is fast, you will automatically handle more info bytes, and keep the "overload" situation away from you.

An important weak link that can affect you is your physical fitness. Lower fitness levels directly affect your ability and performance. On a day with lady luck on your side, even though unfit, or at a lower threshold of fitness, you may get away with any kind of situation / mission without a mishap. But when she deserts you, coping with emergencies without peak mind-body combination at your disposal, you will suddenly understand the truth that this one track mind was never designed for the complexities of flight. Generally, Lady Luck does not desert you completely or the situation is "not so grave." Mostly, such a combination exists daily for a vast majority of us. This feeds the false premise that "it can't happen to you" and that you can get away again and that you are the lucky one / the chosen one. Beware, "gravity" can increase suddenly and Lady Luck can sometimes upstick and leave.

Remember, you have to not only maintain within the aircraft design limitations, but also within your physiological and psychological limitations. Unless you know your own limits, performance errors will occur. You can definitely enhance your own mind-body envelope by increasing your knowledge levels, skill levels, and keeping yourself physically fit. These will enhance the possibility of a good decision from you – in spite of the one track mind. ❑

# A Little Foreplay

What does a fighter pilot, currently out of the "hot seat", on a staff job do? Reminisce, naturally. But the cronies and the comfort of the crew room are absent. Even the bar is a hostile territory – filled with unknown faces. So, armed with a pencil and an eraser (a combination mightier than the pen), he takes refuge in writing nostalgia.

Ah! The good old days. Each dawn was greeted by the roaring sound of piston engines being warmed up, turn by turn by the "Chiefy" and his "boys". When the pilots arrived after the Met brief, the aircraft would be ready for flying. As time went on and the pistons retreated, this scene was recreated only at Training Command and the transport bases – the only ones with pistons on them. The fighter bases had been re-equipped with the "fast" jets which didn't need such "foreplay", in the form of "warm up" prior to action. They didn't need any "petting" after the sortie in the form of a proper "cool down cycle" either. Very business-like and appealing to the male psyche. And, of course, these jets were of European stock. Oh! To be in England!

Could the bliss last? Naturally, not. The Russian technology made its entry into the Indian flight line through the MiG-21s. The Russian jet engine preferred the "foreplay" like the piston engines of yesteryears. It even demanded an "afterplay" in terms of a proper cool down cycle prior to switch off. Once again, dawn at the MiG-21 bases was greeted by the roar of "warming up" MiG engines. Used to the no nonsense way of the European jets, the "foreplay" demanded by the Russian jets was felt to be of only nuisance value and was accepted till the "shine" and the "newness" of the MiG-21s remained. Slowly, the easy ways asserted themselves, practices forgotten / changed, the "warm up" habit given up for good and the cool down cycle invariably ignored. Well, the engines and our body have a lot in common. A warm up prior to a rigorous work-out, and a cool down cycle immediately after it are ignored only by the foolish. The damage, both for the body and the engines surfaces later, when the cumulative effect piles up. But more of that later.

MiG-23s were inducted in the Indian Air Force (IAF) in 1980. Their engines were shown scant respect, with no warm up or cool down cycles for ten years. One of these R-29 engines quit in sheer disgust in December 1990. In fact, it was so angry, like a lady scorned, that it just exploded on the take-off point. As if to reinforce the point, another R-29 engine followed suit a little later. The MiG-27s were treated similarly and one of their engines, a cousin of R-29, responded in exactly the same fashion. The Russian specialists were consulted and they pointed their finger at the total infidelity to the warm up cycle. Once this practice was resorted to, the situation took a turn for the better.

Meanwhile, flame-outs after start up or while taxiing increased on the MiG-21s. The Russians again insisted on warm up and cool down cycles. But the sceptics pointed out that MiG-21s have been here for decades without a problem. So why introduce a nuisance! Mr Nusberg – the famous engine specialist from the MiG Design Bureau – then gave details of why we must follow warm up and cool down cycles on MiG-21s. The gist is given below:

- Without warm up, components may eventually disintegrate due to cumulative thermal strain.
- Inadequate warming up of the combustion chamber leads the way to twists and warps which may induce shift of flame pattern, incomplete combustion of air and fuel mixture, increased carbon deposit, burning

and failure of flame tubes, and, finally, to overheating of turbine blades.

- Changes in the performance of the combustion chamber may lead to changed air flow, resulting in engine surge.
- Absence of warm up cycle increases friction loads and this would entail failures of seals and other components in the long run.
- The warm up cycle helps in reducing radial clearances in the compressor and turbine, thus, augmenting efficiency and thrust.
- Thermal strains and excessive radial clearances may lead to engine surge.
- The viscosity of the oil of a non-warmed engine is higher, leading to poorer lubrication. This would lead to failure of seals and emergence of chips in the oil.
- Ignoring the cool down cycle may lead to development of thermal strains, and cause overheating of fuel. Fuel acts as a lubricating agent for fuel system components and overheated fuel loses its lubricating properties. This may further lead to rpm fluctuations, decrease in pump output, temperature overshoots, and may result in surge and flame-out.
- After shut down of the engine, the heated components of the air duct are encompassed in cold ambient air, causing high thermal strain. To rule out such phenomena, compulsory cooling down cycles for two minutes at idle rating is called for.

Frightening, isn't it? "If I had known all this, I would never have ignored the warm up and cool down cycles on MiG-21s." Did I hear someone say this?

The orders to carry out both the warm up and cool down cycle on MiG-21 aircraft exist, but implementation is slowly losing its fervour and people are beginning to ignore them. It is hoped that this backgrounder would succeed in making these acts a little more meaningful and less irritating to perform. Like the foreplay. ❑

# Romance of the Night

Night invariably brings in visions of romance. For a pilot, especially a fighter pilot, it is night flying which ushers in romance. It beckons him, for it has challenges that are an enigma to him. I can still recall the first time I flew at night as a cadet. Those days the aviation medicos hadn't yet gotten over the red light vs rods for vision adaptation at night. So the crew rooms, flight office and the surrounding area were lit red; not with red bulbs but by red paper on normal bulbs – the handiwork of 'duty cadets'. The complete atmosphere with that strange glow had a 'different' feeling. It immediately transported one to a special elite crowd whose world view was not the mundane earth-bound-tied to-reality kind. Instead, one revelled in its "eliteness", defying gravity, and loved to live life a little unreal.

Night flying is the art of flying made trickier and more complex, with traps at each step. Speed is assessed by the rate at which the navigation light travels over the goose necks. Depth is a concept you try to grope around for with the control column, so that you can fathom its dimensions. Slowly, one masters it all, including the tricky swing of the piston engine on take-off and the more difficult three pointer landing. The first night solo is truly an exhilarating experience. Up amidst the stars all alone! Wow! The thought of a good landing pumps in the requisite adrenaline and true to one's instructor's hopes, Mama's prayers and one's personal ambition, a good landing is pulled off.

I slowly graduated to being a supersonic night fighter pilot. Exercises at night were then not too difficult and most of the flying was done at height. Compulsory usage of 100 per cent oxygen had already complicated the scenario with the remainder of the night, in bed, made difficult with weird sounds in the ear. A drink after night flying was a must then. It was the-done-thing and so one did it. It's only now that I know how it helps my body to uncoil and relax sufficiently to permit sleep. In fact, those days, the Aviation Medicine lectures revolved mainly around the middle ear, hypoxia and night adaptations vs red light. Disorientation was not a much touted word.

'Fascination', 'empty field myopia' GLOC and a host of such terms crept in much later.

Night flying soon became commonplace and some of its challenge lost its shine and naturally wouldn't produce the bounce on the pitch till one went on leave. On return, one discovered rather quickly that night flying had regained its stature and was once again awe inspiring as one tried to be confident of the touchdown and, instead, found oneself groping for the ground. Or when one encountered clouding while on a PI or a letdown, or some clear air turbulence. One usually developed a healthy respect for the challenges of the night, and like good boys, tried to grab some sleep in the afternoon so as to be "exceedingly fit" for the night mission.

On one such return to night flying after leave, my flight commander took me up for a dual check. The braver of the lot those days took you through aerobatics and always told you not to try them on your own – a sure-fire recipe to ensure that this art was kept alive. Anyway, it was a heady experience for a youngster and when we came in to rejoin from an unorthodox direction, the position in the air was such that only through a double circuit pattern could I get on to correct downwind. Now this was not the normal rejoin method. My mind would not accept the change and I flew the aircraft as if for a normal rejoin. Naturally, the downwind heading turned out to be the reciprocal. I tried again, but got the same result. I just could not solve the problem. The flight commander took over and handed me the controls only on downwind. This was my first encounter of night disorientation or lack of situational awareness or plain stupidity or a total inability at handling geometry at height – call it what you may. I could not believe that such a thing could have happened to me. So, like many self-inflicted insults and injuries, it was promptly forgotten.

The mid-seventies saw a change with 25 per cent of the task at night becoming a norm and 'Night Strike Syllabus' coming in vogue. The shine returned on the ball as challenges mounted in geometric progression. There were the low level navs, the pseudo-aeros, the range work, and live strikes, all permitted legally on dark nights, too. Suddenly, it was fantastic fun, with competition galore. The fighter pilot blossomed. The romance had matured and marriage appeared on the horizon for there was so much of night flying that it all seemed so easy! A featherbed – this night flying. Where had the challenge disappeared? The demon awaited its turn to strike.

The squadron moved to Jaisalmer on detachment. Complacency had set in, and night flying was given a cavalier treatment. The desert had an eerie silence which could unsettle even the most complacent of us all. On one such night, the winds changed and so did the runway. There was a still a trace of airmanship present in the cocksure ego which prompted one to attempt a practice circuit on the new runway. (No, no, out of the question. So how about a practice GCA and an overshoot! Yeah, that's acceptable). So in the guise of a GCA, a circuit approach was practised. At the round off, height throttle was advanced, the beast roared its might and once again rose to penetrate the sky. Amidst all this macho imagery, the gyros toppled. No, not the ones provided by the Mikoyan Gurevich design bureau but the ones in the head. For outside, the starless sky was the blackest ever possible, with a fish bowl effect giving the feeling that the aircraft was in a steep climbing turn. The instruments were refuting the turn part. The body wouldn't believe them. It took an agonising long battle for the body to wear out before the combined might of the Tumansky engine and a massively brainwashed head which continued to believe in the supremacy of instruments. Only when, a 180° turn later, the lights of Jaisalmer town dazzled for an eternity, did the mental gyros restabilise and stop questioning the instruments. Chastened, and with a bruised ego burdened with an almost bad landing, it was later, with a little help from the bottle, that the battle of the gyros was relegated to the 'dunce corner' at the back of the mind.

Oceanic waves of times erase the impressions made on the beach of flying experience, otherwise the devil of disorientation wouldn't succeed so often. Plenty of night flying later, the episode of disorientation was a forgotten defeat – not available for recall. There is a common belief that a night mission 'a day' keeps disorientation away. Nothing could be more untrue. Read on.

It was again the middle of a good season. With heaps of night flying and regular night strikes, both live and dummy, a dummy strike to a neighbouring base, not below 150m AGL, on a dark night, seemed easy enough. But this fighter pilot hates milk runs. So a new route was chosen to increase the odds and maintain a challenge. The map was studied, course and timings properly committed to memory to offset the odds. The Met briefing showed that the weather God did not like the evenness of the picture and had introduced plenty of clouding and an odd CB slightly displaced from the route. Well, that would keep the stars out, and the only lights would be those of the villages and towns. "No, Sir, there would be no lights below either. This is desert at ten pm." Thus, fully prepared, mentally and physically fit, rides out our charioteer: "On course and time at the first turning point" reported the radar. A little further away, the radar refused to acknowledge the voyager's path as it was out of its orbit. No sweat. 'Sit' under control. Halfway on the second leg, the clouds appeared closer and closer. Now they are touching the canopy and then the famous ventral fin of the MiG-23. It is not turbulent at all. The thrill has returned with full vigour and the adrenaline can be felt. There is no question of deviation or return. The fighter pilot is wedded to the accomplishment of his mission, and such thoughts, when they appear, are quickly swept away. The little voice of airmanship tries to make itself heard by such inane statements, "Listen, it's a dark night, low, dark clouds abound, CBs are in the neighbourhood, abandon the mission." The ego is too full of its own voice and this advice of the "little airman" is ignored / treated with contempt. It makes one last attempt by stating, "Listen, fella! you are a single ship with no one watching you. So if you bow out sensibly before the weather, no one will question you." The ego responds, "Questioning my integrity, are you?" The little voice is rebuked into absolute silence. And the mission continues for another ten minutes. The clouds give way and one sees the lights of a township nearby, second TP on time. On the third leg, it's IMC again. Two minutes in the clouds and suddenly one is blinded by a dazzling display of colours and light a little to the left of the track. So bright and so "Diwali-ish". It was as if one of those famous remarkable rockets – no, not the Oscar Wilde variety – but the one from our Sivakasi factories, burst a few feet away. Simultaneously, the mental gyros capsised. Autopilot level mode was engaged while the heart and soul were now locked in a virtual battle with the body to regain orientation. The body wouldn't believe that the aircraft was in level flight. Against all the demands of the body, the autopilot was trusted and relied on for almost ten minutes. The body continued to tell me that I was in a descending spiral to the right. When I broke clouds, the terrain was of no help. A little while later on track and on time, I saw the township of my target airfield some distance to my right at 2 o'clock. I altered course to head for it even though it was not supposed to be on my track. Slowly, my mental gyros started stabilising. I could actually sense their agonisingly slow motion towards stabilisation. Only when I came overhead did my body gyros resemble the AGD readings. Needless to add, the target was struck within the permissible variation of two minutes. The fighter pilot triumphed, but how.

The return leg was scheduled at a cosy altitude of 5 km. This was achieved in a zoom. A lovely scenario was unfolding ahead. Stars twinkled above. There was complete darkness below, punctuated by clouds and some lightning. Well, none of it was on my track. Thanks to the autopilot and long return leg, I had time enough for introspection. What caused the disorientation? Dancing, dazzling, "Diwali-ish" display to upset the daring hero of the night? Could it be a UFO, a meteor or merely the Army Gunners enjoying an off-season Diwali? I was never to know. What I did learn was that when the body chemistry is flushed with confusion about orientation, immediately embrace the level mode of the autopilot and you will live to see and hear the other side of the Pink Floyd moon. And the romance of the night will continue. ❑

# Situational Awareness

Situational Awareness (SA) is the favoured flavour of the season. As jargons go, this one too has many shades, mostly misunderstood. It is the latest peg on which to hang your flight safety hat, the latest panacea that will drive away all ills. Its presence produces beatific smiles, with Nirvana written all over the forehead. A term that is flogged regularly in briefings/debriefings, crew rooms and even in Commanders' Conferences.

In my younger days as an aviator, it was the term "airmanship" that held centrestage and all paid obeisance to it. It encompassed everything. Slowly, it lost its glitter and the lexicons began to ignore it. I am not sure how or why this good term lost its value. May be too many rules, too many long winded briefings and debriefings, and the ascendance of the legal mind who kept asking, "Where is it written?" probably sounded its death-knell. It slowly receded into the background and even Presidents, enquiring into flying accidents chose not to talk about it or even mention it.

Then arrived "situational awareness" whose presence or absence became the foundation stone of many arguments discussing flight safety. I have even heard demands that SA be taught. Heading a prestigious institution of learning, I thought it best to put on record what I think situational awareness is.

Situational awareness is ubiquitous and permeates all walks of life and can be applied everywhere. I would restrict my arguments to the flying environment where this term finds most usage. As one progresses in life, one learns many skills. Walking, running, cycling, swimming and driving are some of them. Flying, a complex skill, takes you to the third dimension. Whenever one approaches any of these skills for learning, initially, the mind-body combination gets fully immersed in picking up the skill. As one gains more experience or gets more skilled, so to say, more of the mind is left free for other tasks. In fact, a stage comes when one feels that these skills are performed by the individual more or less automatically.

Comes an emergency or a complex situation – the mind again gets absorbed in handling the situation, no longer free for these other tasks. Have you noticed that when there is extra traffic on the road or you want to overtake someone in dense traffic, you stop talking / whistling / humming and tend to switch the car stereo off! This is because you want your mind to be free to tackle the expected complex situation. Let me use an analogy. In our mind, each one of us has a computer. When we begin learning a skill, the mind's computer is so saturated in handling the skill that it has absolutely no space for handling any other task. As our skills improve, the mind's computer is able to relegate these skills to one corner of its hard disk and a lot of space is freed for handling other tasks. The more skilful a pilot, the greater will be his ability to handle other bits of information, as the space on his computer will be larger for processing other bits of info. An experienced pilot, for example, will almost automatically apply backward pressure on the stick when the aircraft descends below the planned flightpath and open throttle if the speed is reducing. A trainee pilot, on the other hand, will have to think it through before applying corrections. Once these skills are learnt, the space on the mind's computer is released for other activities like navigation, monitoring fuel, R/T calls, handling emergencies, etc. If the pilot is comfortable in the cockpit, fully aware of the surroundings, only then will he have free space on his mind's computer. It is this computer space which holds the key to situational awareness. During my instructional tenure at Hakimpet, 27 years ago, I had a pupil (cadet) who, with just 30 hrs under his belt, was able to detect a wrong homing (180° out) given by the ATC as he could co-relate it with his ground position. His situational awareness was phenomenal. This was so because he was a gifted flier and, thus, had extra free space on his computer for other tasks, while his course-mates – my other pupils – used it all for coordinating mind and body for flying the aircraft. They would have responded mechanically to such an R/T call. Similarly, a pilot who knows his emergencies well will have more computer space for SA. Another pilot who has practised his emergencies and situations on the simulator will have yet more space available for SA. A tired or fatigued pilot's SA is bound to be lower as either his computer space would have shrunk or his piloting skills may be occupying more of the available space. Similarly, a pilot who flies after a long break would find a similar lowering of space for SA till he regains currency. A person with better knowledge of rules and regulations, of procedures, of diversionary airfields, of the environment, etc is bound to have more space for SA as his mind is that much freer for information processing and decision making.

Is SA tangible? Can it be taught? I don't think so. We can only create conditions for the presence of good SA. High levels of skill, knowledge and experience, when coupled with a fit mind-body combination at an optimum level of arousal, will give us the best chances for the presence of good SA. One must not chase SA. What need to be chased are the other ingredients whose presence will automatically produce SA. ❑

# The Dreamer

The first sketch that he ever made in his life was of an aeroplane. It was sort of natural, too. For he was born amidst fighter pilots. His father is that rare breed that defies the heavens day in and day out. All his senses were overwhelmed with fighter aircraft. When he looked around as an infant, he saw and heard aircraft taking off, landing or just over-flying his dwellings. When his tiny hands reached for his Papa, it was either Papa returning from his sorties in his fancy but sweaty flying overall or going to work in a uniform whose colours, wings and ribbons fascinated him no end. No wonder then that he dreamt of becoming a "Fighter Pilot". Proud of his profession, this gladdened his Papa's heart and increased the worry lines on his Mama's face. Each day of her married life was filled with prayers that every one of her husband's take-offs must equal a landing. A not too infrequent slip in such an equation, at many flying stations that she had lived on, had partly jolted out the sense of adventure and the glamour associated with her husband's profession. Its place had been taken by a vacuum which was filled only when her husband returned safely from his flying. Now her son wanted to follow in the footsteps of his father. All her worry lines melted into a smile at the thought of her husband who came back each day after flying, so happy and contented. Where else will you get paid for what you enjoy doing? She won't come in the way – she reasoned – it is indeed a noble profession. Let the son carry on the tradition if he wants to. God will take care of the rest.

Already obsessed with flying at the age of six, he returned one day from school and announced to his Mom that his eyes were the best in class. While others scored a mere 6/6 in the eye test, his score was 6/9. Shocked by this news, an ophthalmologist was immediately consulted, who confirmed it. He opined that the source was genetic and the eyesight would continue to reduce till his growth stopped. How cruel ! How would he fly with spectacles?

In one swift blow, the dream of the child lay shattered. Or so we thought.

His fascination for aircraft nevertheless, continued to grow. While his classmates filled their rooms with posters of heroes of the sports world, his room was a virtual collage of the world's fighter aircraft. His recognition skills of aircraft and knowledge on flying left many experts surprised. How does one tackle such enthusiasm! One tried to gently tell him that he should now refocus or rechannelise such enthusiasm towards achievable goals. Flying was out for him. The number of the lens on his spectacles at the age of 12 was already minus three. One only shuddered to think of the future of his eyesight. His parents set up a 'persuasion campaign' to wean him away from

flying. Didn't they succeed in getting him to stop sucking his thumb? So, gently, each day, more avenues and better hobbies were discussed. Over a period of time, they got the feeling that the boy had got over his 'obsession'.

One day, he came home with a magazine article on the Russian method of correcting myopia through sharp minute incisions on the eyes. The resoluteness to become a fighter pilot was back in place. Why fight such determination? A visit to Delhi was planned to explore the viability of such an operation. After check-ups, the doctors explained that this operation was done after a child's growth stopped. So our young man planned his operation for 19 years of age. Simultaneously routing via the National Defence Academy (NDA) was abandoned in favour of a direct entry to the Air Force Academy as the entry age there was higher. His walk now possessed an extra bounce that God gives to feet that are sure of their route and the destination.

Then came the rude shock. On his biannual eye check-up, the Air Force eye specialist mentioned that the Armed Forces have not accepted the Russian method of correction, as many cases have been known to regress. Crestfallen, the young dreamer lost his appetite, the bounce and the zest. The smile vanished to be replaced with total gloom. Ma and Pa once again swung into action with another 'persuasion campaign'. Manmohan's magic and the marketplace economics were twisted and turned to show their glitter from every angle so that the glamour of flying paled in comparison. The sheer breadth of scope for careers available today was explained. All greeted with muted response, more in deference to the efforts put in by his parents than to any change of opinion or heart. Inwardly, they too suffered with him, for he was merely dreaming their dream.

Slowly, over the years, the change started showing. The posters in his room were now of Brooke Shields, Sabatini and others of their ilk, stars in their own firmaments. The lad no longer talked of flying in the same vein. His wistful gaze at an over-flying aircraft lacked the intensity of the bygone days. At last, the boy had grown into an adult.

Recently, he charged into the room with another article – removal of myopia with laser rays. This time, the methodology's origin was in the US of A – the Mecca of inventions. The article claimed that this kind of operation, though expensive, had none of the drawbacks of the Russian method. And it would soon be available in India. Hope triumphed. Brooke Shields posters were dispatched to Agassi, Sabatini's to his tennis loving friends and F22s and Su 30s once again adorned his room walls. His bouncy gait returned, plans of routing to the Air Force Academy resurrected, and the smile firmly back where it belonged.

Will God be unkind again? The dreamer and his parents fervently hope and pray not.

P.S. The above was written in 1993. Eye correction through laser surgery is still not accepted for military aviation. The "dreamer" then became a software engineer whose hobbies include flying. ❑

# Address to Cadets

All of you have been through the Services Selection Board. A lot of you must have been asked the question "Why do you want to join Air Force?" Many of you may have said "To serve the nation; / to defend the country / to serve the motherland." Some of you may have understood the real meaning of this answer but to a large number amongst you, the answer may have been used as it 'sounds' or appears

the most appropriate. Whatever may have been the rationale for the answer – the reality is that you are here in the Air Force Academy, on the springboard of a career that will test your answer regardless of whether you meant it or not. How does one defend the nation? Not by saying that I will defend the nation but through ACTION. And what are these acts and how do you perform these acts that will enable you to do what you said – defend your nation? By upgrading yourself physically, mentally, emotionally and psychologically to a level where you do not hesitate to produce the supreme sacrifice – of laying down your life for your country. It is this upgradation of you at the physical level, at the mental level, at the emotional and psychological level we will be attempting here at the

Academy. So that all of you change over from a civilian to an AIR WARRIOR. Who, when called upon, without hesitation delivers the knockout punch to the enemy.

Some of you, who have joined the supporting services like Administration, Logistics, Education, Accounts, etc, must be wondering how are you connected to the AIR WARRIOR. Well, the nature of warfare has changed. Once upon a time, war was limited to the borders, and the Air Force fought a very clean battle from bases that were far from the borders. Only the aircrew went across to enemy territories. The engineers and other supporting services stayed back at the airfield. All that has changed with the nature of warfare having changed. Today, there are no borders. Witness the terrorist, deep in the USA, and us in India, who have been facing such threats for a very long time. The enemy is right here – amidst us. So your first war starts when you have to defend yourself against terrorists. And how do you do that. First, upgrade yourself at the four levels that I mentioned.

Upgrade yourself so that you become air warriors. With all the embellishment that a soldier has. Thereafter, comes your specialisation or the branch. Even there you have to view the Air Force like the body. Just as the body will function below par when some of its organs don't perform, the same goes with the Air Force. An important lesson here is that each organ is equally important for the body. Without the heart or brain, the body fails, but with both these available, and no hands, you can't deliver the knockout punch. Therefore, don't compare and think of other branches as less than yours but view them as part of the same body called the Air Force. Wherein each branch has its specific role to play.

Each branch is important and only together can we deliver the knockout punch with precision. ❑

# Flight Safety and Operational Effectiveness

(Extract from Keynote Address - IFSCON 2007)

As *homo-sapiens* evolved, their prime occupation of hunting kept them constantly focussed on locating food resources. Thus, for thousands of years, our ancestors remained nomadic and led a very unstable life. It was only when agriculture was discovered that man began settling down. It took almost ten thousand years for the industrial age to dawn. Two centuries later, the Wright brothers got airborne and the world changed dramatically. The advent of aviation has transcended all barriers and has rocketed man into space as well. Today, aviation and space exploration have changed man's environment totally.

Till aviation made its arrival, we remained isolated and cocooned as individual nations and people. The huge landmasses, with their hostile conditions, created daunting chasms. The oceans created an abyss that was hazardous to cross. Thus, interaction between societies was limited. But aviation changed the situation completely. Aviation has shrunk the world and made the global village possible. Aviation has ushered in globalisation that has spread rapidly across continents. It is time to maximise on opportunities that have become a reality today, and derive and share the benefits from each other. History also teaches us that those civilisations of the past that remained isolated and cocooned were soon decimated by the ravages of time and are all but remembered. It is precisely with this in mind that the concept of IFSCON and its theme, Aviation Safety, A Universal Language was synthesised. The conference focusses on meaningful interaction of experienced flight safety functionaries of a spectrum of Air Forces of the world and associated civilian aviation organisations under a common umbrella.

Flight safety is an ongoing concern for all organisations and personnel involved in aviation. In recent times, significant progress has been made in the field of flight safety in terms of new ideas, methods and techniques developed for aircraft accident prevention and investigation. Aviation safety is being treated as a management function. Aviation organisations are accepting new programmes and adjusting them until they work efficiently. Concepts and approaches such as "System Safety", "Quality Assurance" and "Just Culture" have gained wide acceptance.

The Indian Air Force has gained considerable experience operating a wide spectrum of aircraft of varied technological vintages. Its flight safety strategy has evolved from a reactive strategy to a proactive one. While undergoing rapid modernisation, the Indian Air Force is continually tackling and adopting these multi-faceted techniques to enhance flight safety, through risk management and technological evolution. Juxtaposed to this scenario is the exponential growth in the civil aviation sector in South Asia, with several new low cost operators taking to the skies. This swift expansion will add tremendous strain to the air space, infrastructure of airports, ground radars, etc. This adds a new dimension to aviation safety and its impact needs to be assessed and addressed by an integrated approach.

Having said this, I would now like to share some of my views on the shape of things to come in the future, issues that we need to deliberate, reflect and ponder upon. Let me take you on a little detour into the past to the days of the birth of air power. The aeroplane took to the air, thus, heralding a new era in the history of military prowess. The aeroplane catapulted air power to the forefront as the dominant and decisive factor in warfare. Visionaries like Douhet had already propounded theories on the impact that the aircraft was destined to have. The overwhelming and devastating effect of the aeroplane overshadowed the losses that were being incurred early on. In hindsight, one can express that there was no concept of safety then. It was only in the post-World War II era that countries became concerned about the high attrition being levied while operating their aeroplanes. The economic factor, the irretrievable loss of the human resource, etc were becoming a matter of concern that countries could not afford to turn a blind eye to. The post-World War II period saw nations take a holistic view of the grim situation and acknowledge the fact that safety in conducting operations needed to be given importance and priority. Thus, it was around the mid-forties and early fifties that Air Forces around the world started taking flight safety seriously. And it was from this period onwards that the accident graphs for most Air Forces started showing downward trends. But does that mean air power has turned safe and assumed a secondary role in dominance? No. All it means is that nations realised that air power and its resources were too valuable to be frittered away carelessly.

The uniqueness of military aviation stands out distinctly. It is driven by mission-accomplishment, is extremely expensive and each loss is exorbitantly difficult to accept. Each accident that we sustain has long-term ramifications. It not only erodes our mission-accomplishment and operational capability but also entails an irreplaceable loss in the human resource as well. Therefore, we need to maximise efforts to prevent such a loss. This naturally implies that flight safety has to be embedded into our operations so as to become integral to mission planning and execution.

One needs to understand very clearly that flight safety and operational effectiveness cannot be segregated into two individual entities. Safety remains an integral component of operational efficiency. I will narrate a personal example of my experience while attending an international Air Power Symposium recently. I was asked how the Indian Air Force had reduced its number of accidents in the recent past. To this, I had replied that one of the reasons for this reduction in accidents was that the Indian Air Force in the recent past had procured newer technology aircraft which are less prone to accidents. It was with the desire to enhance our operational effectiveness that we acquired assets, which, in turn, had given us the high-end technology that had a positive result in our flight safety record. It is because flight safety and operational capability are deeply interwoven that each complements the other. ❑

SECTION – II

# OPERATIONS

# Decibels at a Fighter Base

Living daily at an Air Force airfield where fighters are based is an experience by itself. There is a continuous roar of fighter aircraft. But one gets used to the differing noise levels and slowly learns to distinguish the very sounds that make up the day and the night. The mighty roar of a lion is what a fighter aircraft taking off sounds like. The roar lasts but a few seconds, for, as the fighter ascends, the vast sky absorbs the roar and silence descends. But fighters rarely operate singly. They do so mostly in formations. The sounds of take-off then are different. The first of the formation lets out a roar and unleashes itself from the bonds of us earth-bound creatures. The next one pauses, as if in respectful silence for the religious ceremony to be over and then lets out his roar of freedom. This continues till the complete formation lifts off, to be reduced to a speck in the vastness of the sky. And remind us, the earth-bound, of the small place we occupy in the universe.

In stark contrast to the take-off, the landing of a fighter has a measured and assured quality in its low sound – like a warrior returning home after a battle. There is an accompanying whistling sound as the fighter approaches the concrete. Whish, says the fighter as the engine power is reduced prior to touch down. Hesitatingly, yet smoothly, the wheels touch the ground. "Shik" say the tyres when they contact terra firma. And then, unlike airliners, which suddenly break into an awful lot of noise when their reverse thrust is applied for braking, the fighter streams out its beautiful parachute which sort of dances to a tune supplied by the wind which you and I can't hear. Silently, the fighter slows down for the turn off the runway and whistles back to its flight line – a job well done.

One gets accustomed to these sounds and the sounds settle down in the subconscious of women like me whose husbands are fighter pilots. But there is one sequence of sound and silence that gets the heart working overtime with anxiety. On a fighter base, when suddenly all sounds cease abnormally

OH MY GOD! WHY HAS
FLYING STOPPED??...ANY MISHAP??!!....
ANY PROBLEM???....I HOPE....
THANK GOD!
THAT ROARING HAS
FINALLY STOPPED!
GOT YOU...AH!!
-DAYAL PRED-

and an eerie silence follows, then ears perk up for the swhish-swhish of the rotor blades of a helicopter. If no such sound comes, one begins to wonder, "Why has flying stopped?" and remains slightly uneasy. But if the air slicing chopper continues its monotone and slowly fades out, then the heartbeats are difficult to contain within the chest walls. For this is the rescue chopper heading for the scene of trouble. A thousand questions flash in a moment. Who's in trouble? Is he safe? A thousand prayers float up as if to tell the Almighty that these fighter pilots dare the elements day in and day out, please let no harm come to them. Mostly, such prayers are answered and heartbeats restored to their normal pace. At times, sadness descends for one of the tribe is no longer amongst us. But this tribe of the brave cannot be contained for long. For soon, as if the sky is a stage and the show must go on, the sound of a fighter taking off resumes its normal place in this high decibel world of an air base and normalcy returns.

Heartless tribe of the brave who mourn their dead so little! No, this brave tribe of fighter pilots is not heartless. Life is. ❑

*(As told by Sangita Verma)*

# The Robot in You

Not so long ago, you learnt to drive. It was an exhilarating experience. Initially, you were so involved in acquiring the "motor skill" (pun intended) that all your attention was focussed on the basic act of driving. You were not aware of the surroundings, the oncoming or the overtaking traffic, the cross-roads, the noise, etc. Slowly, it settled down. You could then drive comfortably, look ahead, monitor the traffic, look out for impending disasters and take decisions to avert them by slowing down/changing lanes/stopping or whatever was necessary. Your skill improved and then you began enjoying the music spun out by the car stereo. How did this evolution take place?

A similar story unfolds when you try to acquire flying skills. In the beginning, you are involved with your 'heart and soul' in acquiring the basic flying skills. There is no time to even comprehend the instructions broadcast on the R/T channel unless it is specifically directed at you. Even when it is, many times you miss the import. Then, slowly, it all settles down. Hands and legs move automatically, R/T calls responded to, situations handled expertly and there is enough time to admire the earth and the sky and the clouds and what not. How did this evolution take place?

The obvious answer is that you learnt the skills, in the first case, driving skills, and in the next, flying skills. Sounds simple. Let us complicate the issue. How does one acquire such skills? It will be worthwhile to understand the mind-body interaction that is involved here.

Broadly speaking, each of us has a personal robot in us. We programme the robot with motor skills. Once the programme is loaded, all one has to do is to 'run' it. The robot then performs all the functions necessary for execution or the performance of the skill. All you do is sit in the car, insert the ignition key, and the robot takes over. Your mind may be elsewhere but the car will move forward and accelerate, the gears will change, steering will keep the car on the road. Basic motoring will continue. God has gifted each of us this robot so that our mind is left free to take charge of other inputs, the traffic, the route, etc. This robot is put to use from the very early stages in our life – when we learn to walk, run, swim, cycle, etc. When the skill is being learnt, the mind is preoccupied with the process of acquiring it, which I term as programming the robot. Once the skill is learnt / robot programmed, the mind is able to tackle other issues. So far so good.

If this robot is gifted to us by God and it handles all motor skills, surely flying too will be handled by it. Yes, except that motor skills form an essential, but only small, part of what we call "flying". Flying entails much more

Now let us relate to this robot in a little more detail. I am sure, while driving, many of us have unconsciously changed into the wrong gear, pressed the brakes instead of the accelerator, honked the horn without intending to. All these probably happened when your mind was elsewhere, or not totally

on the job at hand. But if your personal robot is supposed to do all these, why do you need your mind on the job too? Or does this robot not follow the ground rules laid down by Isaac Asimov? Or does the programme that you inserted in the robot get infected by a virus or get corrupted? Well, yes and no. When your robot handles or mishandles these activities on the ground, the risks are minimal. Remember, you are on the ground. But in the air, the odds get heavily stacked against you when this robot misbehaves. That this robot, generally well behaved, at times decides to do something other than what we ordered is not recognised by us. What we must understand is that the robot needs constant MONITORING. You may have heard / read about so many pilots who were sure they carried out vital actions on downwind but landed

without wheels, undercarriage lever selected up instead of flaps, mixture control moved instead of throttle, etc. The basic point here is that this robot needs MONITORING. You can initiate the programme of the robot but must keep returning to check that the right programme is running. The robot is known to misbehave. At times, it even initiates the wrong programmes. Therefore, the next time you order the robot, check that the right programme is initiated and thereafter return regularly to monitor the programme. Undercarriage and flaps levers are generally located close by and there have been any number of cases when the robot has elected to handle the wrong one even though one's mind gave the correct orders. The result was the embarrassment of the robot's owner and, may be, an incident. Here, the failure lay in not MONITORING the robot.

There is one area where you should not allow the robot in you to function at all. This is the area of VITAL ACTIONS. Vital actions must be done consciously, with full presence, total focus and undivided attention. Do not let your robot enter and take over this activity. Your personal robot has a tendency to creep in and take over the controls. Use your will power and keep him out of this zone. Let him know who is the master. As the title VITAL ACTIONS implies – these actions are far too important to be entrusted to the robot in you.

Your personal robot will perform best when you are at your physical best, with the optimum level of arousal. It is liable to err when you are tired and fatigued or in a state of anxiety. These are some of the occasions that demand that you definitely MONITOR your robot. And most likely you won't. So watch out. Robots get rusty, too. Post your annual leave or ground tenure, you will need to retrain or reprogramme your robot.

Have I made your personal robot into a villain which keeps letting you down? I hope not. He is God's gift to every pilot. Without this personal robot, you will never be able to perform the multitude of tasks that "flying" entails. He is your best friend. Keep him well-honed – but remember, he needs constant MONITORING. ❑

# But I Believe it is Permitted

Nothing can beat an example when it comes to explaining an idea which has not crystallised into a common, well known phrase. So let me start by quoting from the files.

In one inquiry, the pilot who carried an unauthorised item in the rear cockpit of a trainer, which resulted in control restriction, causing an accident, stated, "I am not aware of any order not permitting such carriage. I remember seeing items being carried in the rear cockpit of many types of trainers."

In another case, an unrated pilot was detailed for a ferry in adverse weather. The Flt Cdr stated, "The fleet was grounded. As a result, the renewal criteria for rating could not be achieved and so the rating expired. Command HQs, thereafter permitted ferry of aircraft by unrated pilots. Ever since, unrated pilots have been flying strikes and ferry." Six months had elapsed since recommencement of flying by the fleet. A majority of the squadron was once again rated. Yet, an unrated pilot was detailed for a ferry in adverse weather, with the old assumption that it is permitted.

In yet another case, a pilot in a low level strike sortie at night, authorised for 150m AOL, was flying the sortie actually at 150m on the radio altimeter, without taking the terrain ahead into consideration. Investigation showed that a large number of squadron pilots were under a similar misconception and had been flying in a similar manner.

The extremely curved approach has been known to cause accidents. Yet, each time it does, pilots are surprised that 500 ft of straight-in approach is the authorised minimum. Regulation-wise below this height, wings should be level.

The unit specialised in the ATGM role. Therefore, nap of the earth flying was a regular feature for the pilots. But when passengers are carried, the minimum height is specified as 500 ft. The pilots took five passengers and decided to show them nap of the earth flying – their regular role – unfortunately, with fatal consequences.

What, you may ask, am I trying to say through examples? Some of the sharper ones amongst you may have traced the presence of the title "But I believe it is permitted" in each of these incidents. Look closely and you will see that in each case, formally established boundaries have been crossed, but in each case, the pilot is convinced that what he has done is actually acceptable.

In reality, what has taken place is that due to repeated violation of a rule, it is taken for granted that the rule does not exist or is no longer operative. So, slowly, what may have been a small mistake actually gains wide acceptance. The old timers in the squadron are replaced by new ones, the wrong practice is passed on, and the rule is slowly forgotten.

This malady – mild in appearance – actually hides a very big hazard. It manages to encroach upon safety margins. Take the case of a MiG-21 trainer. We were all taught that unless fuel drops to a certain level, do not carry out an overshoot (by the way, it is written in the Pilot's Notes, too). So each dual check either started with a few aeros or a GCA pattern to get the fuel to a level that is commensurate with safe rollers / overshoots. Someone in a MiG-21 somewhere commenced circuit overshoots immediately after take-off. Many followed this short-cut, forgetting the inbuilt safety margin. Soon, it became an established norm. Till one day, we lost two lives.

Is it possible to overcome this extremely hazardous, "But I believe it is permitted" syndrome? I don't think so. It is a well nigh impossible task, because the potential for such mistaken belief is everywhere. I have throughout illustrated this with examples from the flying fraternity for that is the one I know best. I am sure this malady prevails everywhere, in all walks of life, and permeates all branches and ranks. Since it is so widespread, I think some broad spectrum antibiotic is needed. I have a few suggestions.

Know thy rules. More importantly, know the why of the rule. Automatically, the safety margin will surface and not merely be a by-product of "OG-ness." Isn't that how we are supposed to differ from the foot stamping brethren of our senior Service? Second suggestion is, be aware of this disease and if it raises its ugly head in your area of operations, ruthlessly chop its head, no matter how small the provocation. Lastly, if you believe there is a rule whose time is past and it is not serving any useful purpose, don't break it but take it up with authorities who are empowered to change it. After all, you may be in that chair tomorrow, or may have just vacated it for a field assignment.

So next time someone tells you, "But I believe it is permitted," I am sure you will be better equipped to deal with this menace. ❑

# The Captain's Predicament

## Brief Narrative

On 29 Oct 90, an AN-32 aircraft arrived at Delhi to take 1.8 tons of service load to Sulur. The aircraft lined up on the runway, and on completion of checks, commenced its take-off run. During the take-off roll, the captain felt a vicious yaw. The aircraft got airborne and then sank and landed on its tail and belly, and finally came to a halt, with the engine running. The engines were switched off with the help of hydraulic toggles. The crew members opened the ramp door and abandoned the aircraft. The aircraft was severely damaged.

## Experience of Crew

The pilot was a Fg Offr with 500 hrs experience on type, and the co-pilot was a Flt Lt with 800 hrs experience on type.

## What Happened?

The calculated VR, V2 and the throttle setting for the load on board for take-off were 215 kmph, 240 kmph and 92° respectively.

The aircraft commenced its take-off roll, with throttle at 92°. Initial acceleration was normal. The navigator commenced calling out speeds from 160 kmph onwards. After 180 kmph was called out, the captain experienced a yaw to the left. He corrected for it with application of rudder and continued without checking or confirming the engine parameters. The captain did not appreciate the loss of power on the left engine even though the acceleration was slow. He rotated the aircraft 'as usual' at 211 kmph against a VR of 215 kmph. At this stage, the aircraft yawed violently to the left. More rudder was applied. The nose wheel lifted up after 4 seconds, but the speed remained around 220 kmph for the subsequent 5 seconds. At this moment, the flight engineer noticed a large fork between the throttles and yelled, "Power." The captain hit the throttles and advanced them to 100 per cent. By then, it was too late. The aircraft had already started sinking. To his horror, the captain found that the undercarriage had already been selected "UP" without his orders. Consequently, the aircraft settled on its tail and then on its belly.

## How did it Happen?

The co-pilot had decided to train his captain by giving him a simulated single engine failure practice. So on take-off roll, he moved the left engine throttle from $92^{\circ}$ to $160^{\circ}$ (flight idle position). To make sure that the captain is "really trained," he diverted the attention of the flight engineer by signalling him to look out for birds. The flight engineer left his seat and went behind the co-pilot to look out for birds on the right. Therefore, when the left engine power was reduced, the flight engineer was not available to warn the captain.

Single engine practice for the captain was not part of the sortie plan, brief or authorisation. Nevertheless, the co-pilot, who had only a little more experience than the captain, felt that he was in a position to impart 'genuine' training to his junior.

The captain did not observe the movement of the throttle, nor did he perceive the loss of power, but he did feel the yaw. He applied corrective rudder and continued with the take-off and rotated the aircraft for unsticking. The aircraft was below VR and, hence, barely got airborne. The co-pilot, to help his captain gain height, cleaned up the aircraft by raising the undercarriage without any orders from the captain. The aircraft sank and touched its tail.

Meanwhile, the flight engineer felt the yaw and then saw that one throttle was at idle rating. He shouted, "Power." The captain, on hearing this, noticed the fork between throttles and immediately opened full throttle on the left engine. The aircraft by this time had settled on its belly.

Abandoning take-off action was then initiated.

## Mistakes Made

The co-pilot, without qualification, competence, authorisation or proper thought, decided to give his captain a practice single engine emergency.

He compounded this mistake by diverting the attention of the flight engineer who could, and should, have helped the captain in handling the emergency.

He made matters worse by raising the undercarriage without being asked to do so and before the aircraft was safely airborne.

If the flight engineer had realised that on take-off his main responsibility was to monitor engine parameters and not birds, he would have noticed the fork in throttles well in time and could have helped avert the accident.

The captain, on noticing yaw at 193 kmph, should have abandoned take-off. He also did not react to the slow acceleration of the aircraft.

## Lack of Crew Coordination

The above incident clearly illustrates lack of crew coordination and understanding. Proper crew briefing and clear-cut role definition would have ensured that the resources available in the cockpit were managed correctly and efficiently. Safety would have followed as a corollary and this highly avoidable accident would then not have taken place. ❑

# From the Files

### What Happened

At a premier fighter base, a young inexperienced pilot made a poor landing, bounced twice and touched third time heavily with a drift. The right tyre burst. The aircraft veered off the runway, rolled to the right and impacted upside down. The aircraft exploded. The crash tenders were activated. The pilot opened his harness QRB but could not come out as the aircraft was inverted and could not be extricated due to the intense fire and, he was burnt fatally inside the cockpit.

### As seen by DATCO

The aircraft toppled and caught fire with heavy smoke. Primary alarm was activated. The CFT-1 (Firex) did not move but the CFT-2 (Tatra) moved towards the crash site at a slow speed. After a few seconds, the CFT-1 (Firex) moved to the crash site. At the site, the Tatra operated foam but it did not reach the fire. Soon thereafter, the CFT-1 (Firex) reached, but no foam operation was seen. A call was given for foam operation on LUP set but no fire fighting was noticed. After a while, the CFT-2 (Tatra) was repositioned on the opposite side of the crash site and fire fighting commenced. The third CFT (Firex) which was in the MT section also reached the site and started fighting the fire.

### As Narrated By NCO I/C Crash Crew

I heard the crash bell. I ran straight to the CFT-1 (Firex) which had its engine started. I told the MTD to move to the site. The Firex crash tender would not move. A second attempt was made but the CFT failed to move forward. The MTD of the CFT-2 (Tatra) was looking at me. I signalled to him to move. The CFT-2 (Tatra) left for site. A third attempt was made to move the Firex, but again it failed to move. Then I jumped into the ambulance and went to the site. At the site, the Tatra had reached, so we operated foam through both the turrets. The throw of the turrets were not reaching the fire, so we tried with one turret only but that too did not reach the fire. So I stopped the operation and asked the MTD to move the Tatra crash tender closer to the burning aircraft. But the Tatra would not move. Meanwhile, the Firex crash tender arrived at the site. I ran to the Firex, entered the cabin and told the MTD to engage the PTO. We tried to engage the PTO, but the CFT failed to operate. Meanwhile, the Tatra moved and had been positioned closer to the burning aircraft. So I came to the Tatra and fought the fire with both turrets and one side line; while this was going on, the third CFT came to the site. I went to it, operated the monitor and side line and fought the fire till it was extinguished. Later, I saw side line of the CFT-1 (Firex) being operated but only water was coming, so I stopped it.

**As Narrated By the MTD of the CFT-1 (Firex)**

I heard the crash bell. I immediately put the gear lever in move position 'D' and on hearing the second bell, I switched on the siren. I put the hand brake off but the vehicle did not move forward. Next, I raised the accelerator slowly, but it still did not move. I changed the gear lever from moving position 'D' to neutral and back three times but the CFT (Firex) still did not move. I switched off the CFT (Firex) and repeated the entire drill again but still the vehicle did not move. On the third attempt, the vehicle moved. I drove the CFT (Firex) to the crash site. There, I was asked to switch on the PTO, but the PTO did not function. I kept on attempting to start the PTO by switching on and off, moving the gear, etc, but to no avail. After a few more attempts, it started working. After completion of the task, I tried to bring the CFT (Firex) back to the crash bay but again it did not move. After some time, it started moving and I brought it to the crash bay. MT fitters were then called.

### As Told By the MT/Fit

On receipt of complaint about the CFT-1 (Firex), I got inside the cabin and started the vehicle, but found the rpm to be very high. So I pulled the accelerator pedal back and brought the rpm down. At this rpm, when I engaged gear, the vehicle moved. I stopped the vehicle and engaged the PTO drive, which also got engaged. So to find out the cause of high rpm, I went out to check the accelerator linkages. I found that the accelerator was connected to both side panels for external operation to aid fire-fighting. The left side panel accelerator was in half-open position. I closed the knob. Now, when the CFT was started, the rpm was at idle, with the gear and PTO functioning normally.

### Availability of Fire Services (Extracts from "Deliberations")

The Station has three CFTs. The Firex has a "known hard steering problem", and the Tatra has very poor pick-up and takes a long time to reach a speed of even 15 – 20 kmph. The third CFT was in the MT section for maintenance but could be made available at short notice.

### As Summarised by the C of I in Deliberations

As soon as the bell rang, the crew took position in the CFT-1 (Firex). When it did not move, the CFT-2 (Tatra) moved and the crew travelled in the ambulance and reached the site. The CFT-2 (Tatra) took 95 seconds to reach the site which was only 400 metres away. The throw of the Tatra did not reach the fire even with one turret. Meanwhile, the CFT-1 (Firex) had reached. So the crew shifted to it but the PTO would not engage. In the meantime, the CFT-2 (Tatra) was manually pushed back and then driven and repositioned. The crew now shifted to the Tatra. The CFT-3 reached at about the time the Tatra started throwing the foam. Part of the crew shifted to it. It must have taken a minimum of 3-4 minutes for the Tatra to start throwing foam from the time the crash bell sounded, and a further 7-8 minutes to put out the fire.

## The Pitfalls

- Both the CFT-1 and CFT-2 had basic problems.
- The Firex has additional throttles outside, on its sides, to aid fire-fighting. If any of these are open, the engine rpm will be high and the gears and PTO will not engage if rpm is above 700. To indicate the engine rpm to the MTD, a rpm gauge is available in the cabin. The MTD was not aware of any of these details.
- The DI card issued to the MTD's vehicles, be it a Maruti van or a Firex CFT, was the same.
- AFSOs had common DI cards for all types and makes of CFTs.

## In-House Search

The above makes very sad reading for it displays a very poor professional approach. It is hoped that the accident details will lead to an in-house search, culminating in corrective measures. ❑

# Standard Operating Procedures (SOPs)

"While towing out a Kiran aircraft from the hangar, it collided with another Kiran parked nearby and damaged its tail plane. Damage repairable at site."

Just four weeks old in my chair as the commandant of the prestigious Air Force Academy, the above accident knocked out my sense of pride, and immediately brought me to ground level. "Wake up, old man. Go out and assess the reality on the ground" my inner voice advised.

So I quickly went to the scene of the accident. Surrounded by eye-witnesses and well-wishers, I was advised that the damage was minimal and the R&SU party at Hakimpet would be able to restore the Kiran to its flyworthy state in a day. There was absolutely no need to report the accident. I heard them all – the supervisors and the operators. Each one trying to minimise the mistakes made and clothe the accident in ordinary apparel. "Just one of those things." "It happens." No attempt to analyse, rectify and improve. Unless the mistakes are recognised, how will one set the stage for improvement ! I asked them to report the accident, and ordered a court of inquiry. The court investigated and blamed the airmen involved in towing the Kiran. My analysis was entirely different. Let me share it with you.

Each hangar has ground markings for parking 12 Kirans safely. The markings ensure safe towing out with a tractor and, hence, the SOP was to park 12. The adjacent hangar was needed for other activities. Therefore, its four Kirans were also added to the 12. So the ground markings for parking were no longer relevant. SOP violated. Did the increase in the number of aircraft parked in the hangar ring any danger bells? Why should it? The aircraft were parked carefully. Did any supervisor foresee that the next day, pulling out these aircraft would pose problems? Did anyone think of increasing the gang size so that more people were available for ensuring safe towing out of aircraft? No one did. Instead, exactly the opposite happened. The personnel detailed for the morning shift were fewer than the daily norm. The stage was set for the accident.

In the initial few weeks of each term at the Academy, there is less flying due its training schedule. Yet, the morning shift was taking out eight Kirans for flying. When the flight commander was asked why he needed eight aircraft, he replied, "But I wanted only two aircraft in the first detail." Only two details of two aircraft were planned by him. Compartmentalisation at its peak, with obviously very poor lateral interaction. Both the operation side and the maintenance side swore that they interacted daily. I was obviously not convinced.

Meanwhile, DSS was readying four aircraft and their preflight servicing was in progress. The next four aircraft were being towed out of the hangar and the collision took place. When one co-related the number of personnel detailed in the morning shift, the tasks at hand and the time-frames involved, there was no possibility of having the minimum stipulated airmen for pulling out the aircraft safely. The situation actually demanded that more

than the minimum stipulated persons be detailed for pulling out aircraft out of the hangar as the aircraft were parked much closer than normal and, hence, more care and help was needed to pull them out safely. Instead, the reverse was happening, with fewer numbers pulling out the stacked aircraft. Is there any surprise that the collision took place?

The chain that led to this accident had many weak links. However, the court of inquiry focussed on the last link – the individuals towing the aircraft out, and blamed them. The other weak links were let off. Needless to say, I intervened and applied the necessary corrective action. Not only to the C of I, but to the complete system at the Academy

This story has many lessons and I am sure the discerning would have gleaned all of them. But let me hammer one very important lesson, lest it go unnoticed by some. SOPs have inbuilt safety margins. Any time you violate any SOP, pause and reflect. Visualise the consequences of your violation of the SOP. The very violation would have squeezed some safety margin. Locate it and then, in your action plan, cater for it.

In the case under scrutiny, the moment additional aircraft were parked in the hangar, violating the safety of ground markings and the SOP, Hangar I/C should have thought about its consequences. If he had, he would have realised that the aircraft would need to be pulled out the next day and would need extra care as they were closely parked. Automatically, more manpower would have been detailed as it was readily available with DSS.

This accident illustrates the pitfall of SOP violation through a ground mishap. Flying activity is full of SOPs and the potential for violating them, both on the ground and in the air, is immense. Each time you violate an SOP thoughtlessly, the accident potential raises its ugly head. It may or may not strike, depending on your luck. If you wish to stay lucky, do not violate the SOP. Life is not perfect and it may produce situations which demand compromise (violation of SOP). In such cases, please compromise "with thought" and not "thoughtlessly".

So, the next time the situation forces you to contemplate violating an SOP, stroll down the cause and effect lane, and visualise what safety margin is getting affected. Cater for it. Flying safety will be ensured. ❑

SECTION – III

# FLIGHT SAFETY: QUALITATIVE ANALYSIS

# Flight Safety Statistics in Perspective

To put the matter of flight safety statistics in perspective, one can group the time periods into the decades of the sixties (1962-71), seventies (19972-81), eighties (1982-91) and nineties (1992-2001). It is seen that the IAF had been averaging a loss of 40 aircraft per year during the sixties and about 30 aircraft per year during both the decades of the seventies and eighties. In the nineties, for the first two years, we are at a figure of 22. It was decided in 1992 that in the nineties, the accidents and the rates have to be halved. How does one achieve it?

To my mind, the only way to pursue this goal is to ignore flight safety – instead "Go for Quality." Flight safety will be the automatic by-product. It should become the endeavour of each individual in the IAF to become "Quality Conscious." Any job that anyone undertakes, he must do it "right, the very first time." If you do your job in the correct, prescribed manner the very first time, irrespective of the temptations, the short cuts, the compulsions, the deadlines, the pressures that beckon you away from the chosen path, you will achieve "quality." And quality will get us our cherished flight safety.

And who will lead the "Quality Race"? Naturally, the commanders in the field. They have to breathe Quality at every step. They have to literally live Quality. Only if they do so, will the message that "the Boss will not accept anything that is shorn of Quality" travel around and permeate the consciousness of our personnel. Once Quality becomes pervasive, Safety will automatically win and we shall stop having unwanted accidents and march successfully towards the goal of halving our accident rates by the end of the decade of the nineties.

Does it sound like a destination! I hope not, for I feel Quality is not a destination just as Safety is not. Both Quality and Safety are journeys to be performed through the way we execute our daily chores and tasks. Do them the right way, the very first time and our days would become more meaningful.

Let us all resolve to become more quality conscious in the standards we set as leaders, and in the execution of tasks as the led. There is a spirit of competitiveness in our country today. One can feel that India is vibrant once more. Let us help it achieve its rightful place in the world by contributing our bit – quality-wise. ❑

# Flying Programme

Whenever I meet anyone from the field, I hear a plaintive cry of being overworked – specially from the flying community. There is a general feeling that tasks have overstretched the existing manpower and the time available. There is so much to do but no time to do it in. In fact, three issues of this esteemed journal last year (Aug, Sep, Oct) devoted a lot of pages to "Time Management." I have a very simple solution to offer. Please read on.

Back in the sixties, the IAF for a fighter pilot in the east was the Garden of Eden. The apple not yet been bitten into. A virtual paradise. Or so it seemed. I was in a Hunter squadron. Working hours were strictly 7:30 to 1:30. Most flying was done at medium / high levels. Bird strikes and green periods, with their impact on flying timings, were quite a few years away. Everyone attended the Station Met Briefing at 7:30. After the Met briefing, the flight commander would reach his office and pick up his flying programme board and a chinagraph pencil. With the aircraft state and the pilot availability information, he would plan the future of the training state of the squadron through the daily flying programme. By 1:30, all aircraft would land, and lunch was invariably on time. Afternoon flying was a rarity and night flying generally non-existent. As the week was a six-day affair, Saturday afternoon was celebration time at the bar. Such celebrations generally extended through the weekend, with Monday coupling again with sobriety. Our neighbours at the base were a Gnat Sqn, a Chetak Unit and an AOP Flight. A similar ambience and routine existed with them.

A real sunshine time. Paradise it was for many years. This peaceful scene was rudely interrupted. Orders arrived from "higher up" that each squadron had to plan its flying a day in advance, and deliver the flying programme to Base Ops by cease work. The fussier AOsC demanded that it reach their office by 1200 hrs. All hell broke loose. "How can I plan flying a day in advance? How do I know how many aircraft will be on flight line? How do I know what the weather will be ? You think these met chaps can predict the weather? How do I know how many pilots will be available? How can anyone know in advance who has to take his wife / children to the Doc? These orders are stupid. These guys in Command forget their days in the field and make irrational demands from us squadron types. There are bound to be changes galore. What is the point of making a plan that has to be changed on an hourly basis? My aircraft serviceability is so poor I just can't predict, then how can I plan? All it will mean is mere waste of time. First plan, and then continuously change." O boy! What a cacophonic reaction reverberated across the width of the IAF.

With hindsight, one can see that the reaction was exaggerated. Planning one's flying a day ahead makes enormous sense. Back then, the advantages weren't so obvious. Management principles were yet to "blip" on the IAF radars. Slowly, planning the flying a day ahead became the norm.

Armament detachments were regular and generally lasted a fortnight. One found that the task was extremely well defined. As the flight commander, I resorted to planning the complete fortnight's plan sortie-wise at the base itself. Armament to be expended was known. Pilot and aircraft availability were less vulnerable to variation at a detachment. The plan invariably went through smoothly. One day, during my tenure as the commanding officer, suddenly I had this bright idea. Why not emulate the detachment fortnightly plan method at the base itself? Did I succeed?

There was a unanimous refusal by both my flight commanders to implement it. Their arguments resembled the uproar witnessed in the seventies when adhoc flying programmes were being replaced with the method in vogue today. They felt that all it will mean is more work as the variables are too many and they will end up carrying out endless amendments. I just could cut no ice with them.

As my style of management at that time was not the steamroller variety, I waited and brought up this issue at the bar, in the party, in the crew room till it became obvious that this CO will not give up. One young supervisor of the squadron probably saw the wisdom and an opportunity, and obliged. Next day, using chinagraph on a huge board in the Nav room, he put down the next fortnight's game plan, sortie-wise, for each day.

There was an immediate uproar. The first thing that all the squadron pilots noticed was that he featured in the maximum number of sorties every day. An immediate protest was lodged with the Flt Cdr, and correction was applied. As the young supervisor was "bright", he had forecast the squadron ambitions / goals correctly.

Did the plan succeed? Of course, there were changes. The usual variables torpedoed a few submarines. But, by and large, it went through. The plan's greatness was in its ability to provide each individual a vast potential to manage his time well. Each one knew when his next sortie would be and what he was planned for. He could prepare his maps / briefings, etc. He could be at his peak mentally and physically to gain the maximum from his sortie. If his planned sortie five days later conflicted with the "Gynec day at MH", the Flt Cdr could oblige him by changing the plan. Others not planned could use their time gainfully rather than just waiting their turn every hour of each day. Because it was put on the Nav Board, the plan was transparent and open to scrutiny. The human angle / bias / partiality were all reduced to the possible minimum. All the goals and targets of Squadron Flying Training were known to all. Both – the squadron pilot and the CO – knew where the operational potential of the squadron was headed. It could be altered or improved, depending on the feedback or the famous "whenever CO desires." We could plan a high low high strike from Jodhpur to Halwara, land, refuel, and then strike Jaisalmer and land back at Jodhpur, all in a day. It was possible to do all the liaison and get all the necessary clearances and tie-ups in this Inter-Command, Inter-SU, Inter-Airfield mission because it was based on a time-frame of a fortnight. Normally, such missions are planned only at the Command level. This could be achieved at the squadron level itself. Such is the potential of a fortnightly flying programme. It even gave ample time to my squadron pilots to carry out the station tasks like Boards of Officers, Courts of Inquiry, etc – tasks somehow seen by an average pilot as earth-bound, demeaning and definitely worth avoiding, specially when time is at a premium. The result – Adjt, C Adm O, AOC all were happy with the "the

Daggers" for "they always delivered". This was in addition to the upsurge in the squadron skill levels on the professional front. A win-win situation for all.

The objections to the plan at the inception stage were due to the imagined impact of the variables. But these can be factored in. The most common variables one has to deal with are changes in aircraft availability and the weather. When one makes the fortnightly programme, both these can be catered for, to a certain degree, as the variables themselves are generally limited and not too enormous. Even when an unexpected change occurs, all one has to do is "tinkering". The changes can easily be absorbed as the basic plan / aim / skeleton already exists. I found that the fortnightly flying programme had many management spinoffs. I, for one, was spellbound by its potential and its fruits. Did it become the norm for the squadron? I was soon posted out and it did not survive my departure. The fortnightly plan demanded clarity of purpose, transparency, fairness and a willingness to sit down and plan. It is so much easier to be fuzzy, partial and do what the whole Air Force does – plan only for the day. I attempted to implement this scheme again when I became the station commander a few years later. I explained the methodology to the CO of the fighter squadron at my base. He would not bite. I tried his flight commanders. They too would not bite. I bade my time and tried it with his successor. He conceded that the idea was very good. That's all. No go again. Unwilling to steamroll, I aborted.

With such marketing failures a decade ago, why am I trying to sell this scheme through the "Flying Safety" pages? I think the time is now ripe for this idea. Each squadron is finding it difficult to manage its tasks. May be this scheme has the answer. Give it a try. The other day, I spent a few hours with a colleague who is in the AEB now. He too opined that our squadrons are full of talented youngsters who are forever running short of time and are "generally harassed". I suggested this idea to him. His eyes and face lit up. His reaction convinced me that I must go fishing again with this idea as the bait. May be someone will bite. He had seen its miniature version, the "Weekly Flying Programme" run by his Canadian counterpart in a foreign Air Force that he had been deputed to. He swore by it. The fortnightly version appealed to him even more for he had seen the weekly version implemented daily as a routine for three years. With obvious benefits and spinoffs.

OK. You still have doubts on this fortnightly flying programme. I give in. At least, try the weekly version. May be the weekly scheme, with its less variables, has more chances of success ! Give it a bash. Once you experience the advantages, do move onto the fortnightly version. Its bite is bigger – I promise.❑

# KBC of Flight Safety

One of the lies that definitely deserves a place in the *Guinness Book of World Records* is the fortnightly red ink entry in each blue book of our squadrons: "Cockpit Blindfold Check and Emergencies Carried Out." Almost nobody does this check but each one records it as having done it. Goebbels' influence can be seen here. A lie repeated consistently and regularly becomes the truth. This scam has been going on for decades. It probably started pretty soon after the issue of the order that demanded that we be checked out in the cockpit for our proficiency with the switches/levers/lights and the way we handle them in mock emergency drills. I was then in the middle batting order of the squadron. Initial enthusiasm slowly gave way to the feeling that we are quite capable in the cockpit and this is all uncalled for. After all, we all fly so regularly. Everybody just assumed that everyone is proficient. Recording it in the bluebook was mandated and a legal necessity. It was treated in exactly that manner and the legal entry placed each week in the blue book. Is the whole fighter population guilty of this misdemeanour?

By and large – Yes. Exceptions only go to prove what the majority does. I too was guilty of it for most of my time. Yet, I consider myself amongst the exceptions who, at least – I'd say once a quarter – enforced the execution of this check in the cockpit. Each time, it brought in the recognition amongst my youngsters that more time needs to be spent by them in the cockpit on the ground practising emergencies. Did they actually do it? I am sure they did not.

Some years ago, my son learnt driving and obtained his driving licence. I had also taught him how to change the wheel. I let him go on a long drive only after he demonstrated his ability to change the wheel. Years passed and as his luck would have it, he never had a flat. Then, one day, he encountered a flat and so needed to change the wheel. He could recall the steps involved but could not remember the exact point where the jack was to be placed beneath the car. Mobile phone and an ever obliging Dad made it easy for him to execute the wheel change and he was back on the road. Why did he forget? He forgot because his memory could not locate this information in its store. Although it was initially stored, my son had never bothered to revise/recall it, hence, memory must have decided that this piece of information was not needed and was, thus, forgotten. On the ground, like in Kaun Banega Crorepati (KBC), the luxury of time, seeking out more information, consulting experts, etc make the job of handling emergencies/situations very easy. In any case, life and death situations are a rarity. Up in the air, the whole ballgame is different. Emergencies occur regularly, very often they need to be tackled in a short time-frame. You can't "phone a friend" and get help. An audience poll is not possible. In fact, life-lines are absent. You have to rely on your own skill and knowledge levels.

Someone up in the aviation hierarchy recognised the basic fact that while flying when you face an emergency, time will always be in short supply. The hands and eyes better move in a coordinated, practised manner. Fumbling and locating switches and levers will only increase the friction in the cockpit whereas a well-oiled, practised response is the need of the moment. And how does one produce this well-oiled response? By practising your checks and emergencies to such a degree in the cockpit on the ground that even when blindfolded, your response is as if the blindfold does not exist. Is this time consuming? Not at all. A few minutes a week will keep you at that level. That is why this order was issued. The validity of this order is well recognised and that is why it was felt that its execution must be recorded fortnightly. If this is so, then how come flight commanders universally fail to ensure its proper execution? It is not that they don't understand its value. It is just that they have many more important chores/issues at hand and they trust the juniors to do this basic activity on their own. What is worse is that no one ever checks the senior pilots in the squadron. They too need this blindfold check. Human nature being what it is, the scene is now pregnant with the possibilities of failures. Suppose one were to suddenly descend on a squadron and subject the youngsters to such a check in the cockpit! Well, I did that once when I was the CO. Most guys just passed muster, a few were proficient and a few were miserable failures. Is this acceptable? Definitely, no. Each and everyone has to be, and MUST be, proficient. Should we try this today in a squadron? I discussed this issue with the DASI inspectors and they informed me that they do this in their inspection at each squadron. On enquiry, they confirmed that test results today are exactly as I had experienced in my squadron almost two decades ago. I again reiterate that this is not acceptable and that each and every pilot, with no exception, MUST be proficient in this test. Will this sermonising motivate you to do this elementary cockpit work? I doubt it. May be if I can make you understand the working of our mind, then may be............

Our mind and body work synergistically. Inputs or information or stimuli are absorbed by our sensory perceptors and supplied to the mind. The mind then processes this information. While processing it, it delves into our "Long-Term Memory Store" to see if it has any "solution" already stored. If found, it is supplied. This then gets translated into action which is executed by our organs/muscles. All this happens sequentially but the time-frames are so minuscule that it all appears like an automatic response. What if the memory store has no solution in its database? The mind will then look for similar situations/models. If not available, it will process the available information/stimuli based on its knowledge levels, and then produce a suitable response.

Research has proved that when you practise your emergency drills in the cockpit, your long-term memory stores it better and for longer durations. Your frequency of practise will dictate how good is the response from this memory bank. The more often you practise recall, the better and faster will be the response. That is why this order has stood the test of time and continues to be valid. You can help the flight commander and yourself by practising the emergency drills in the cockpit without him forcing you to. If and when he checks, display your proficiency and prowess, and surprise him. And the message for the flight commanders – do trust your youngsters but ensure that this weekly blindfold emergency check is done diligently in the cockpit only. The time spent with the youngsters in the cockpit will be a real good investment that will yield compound interest and show up in your safety records. OK, so get into the cockpit now and practise before your flight commander arrives, to check. This practise will provide you the "Life-Line" so that you too can score high on the KBC of Flight Safety. ❑

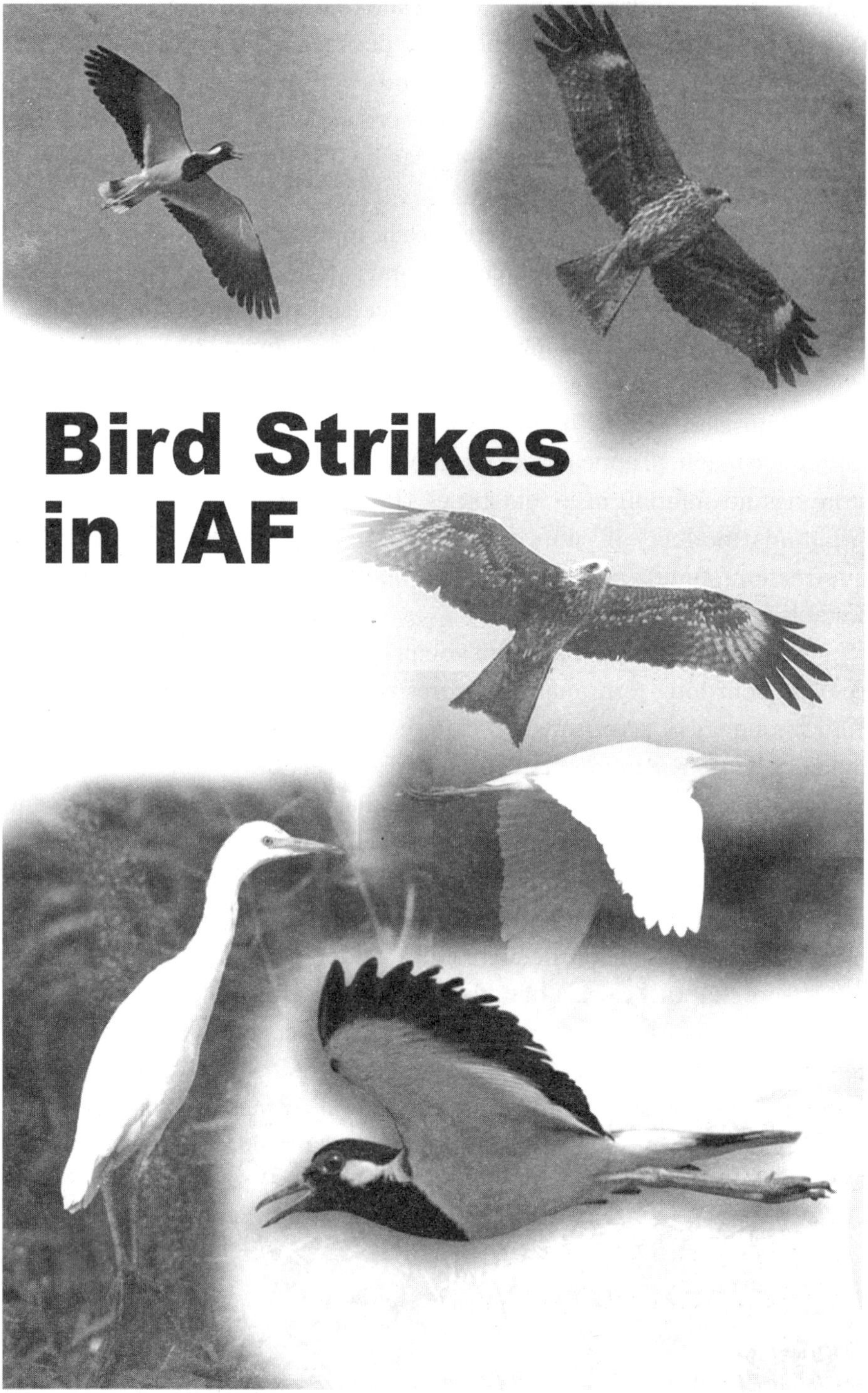

# Bird Strikes in IAF

# Bird Strikes

## Introduction

Historically, the sky belongs to the birds. It was only in the beginning of this century, with the birth of aviation, that we started sharing it with them. Birds outnumber the aviators millionfold and consider it their right to use air space. Man, being the bigger animal, manages to bully them out of their territorial rights. Unfortunately, many a time he has to pay a very heavy price in terms of losses of aircraft and lives.

The first known case of a bird strike was in 1910 in the USA when a seagull got caught in the control cable of an aircraft which then crashed. With the increase in speed, the type and extent of damage too changed its shape. The force of impact is directly proportional to the square of the velocity at collision, e.g., an aircraft at a speed of 250 knots hit by a 2 lb bird would produce an impact force of 178,000 foot pounds. So the enormity of the damage can be gauged. In transport aircraft, redundancy in all systems is high and, hence, the effect in terms of losses of aircraft and lives is contained. This is so with civil aviation. In military aviation, with the bulk of its force consisting of fighters and fighter bombers, where, by virtue of the design factors, inbuilt safety margins are much less, bird strikes pose a major problem. Most fighter aircraft in our inventory are single engined and a bird hit severely damaging the engine invariably implies an ejection, resulting in aircraft loss. And in case the hit is on the canopy, it may lead to pilot incapacitation and then, perhaps, loss of a pilot too.

## Statistics

Let us have a look at the statistics. The IAF, from 1989-94, has recorded the following number of bird hits:-

| | |
|---|---|
| 1989-90 | 144 |
| 1990-91 | 107 |
| 1991-92 | 99 |

| | |
|---|---|
| 1992-93 | 100 |
| 1993-94 | 102 |

The number of aircraft lost in these years is:-

| | |
|---|---|
| 1989-90 | 4 |
| 1990-91 | 1 |
| 1991-92 | 1 |
| 1992-93 | 4 |
| 1993-94 | 3 |

Many a times, the engine is damaged but the aircraft manages to execute a safe landing at a nearby base. The number of engines lost in the five-year period is as follows:-

| | |
|---|---|
| 1989-90 | 47 |
| 1990-91 | 30 |
| 1991-92 | 31 |
| 1992-93 | 32 |
| 1993-94 | 40 |

Month-wise distribution shows that the months with the maximum number of bird hits in the past are September, October, November and February. These months are also associated with "good visibility" and clear weather. So, a lot of flying, by both birds and aircraft, is a natural corollary.

Time-wise distribution indicates that maximum bird strikes take place between 0700-1100 hrs; this period also coincides with maximum flying activity. It is seen that there is no time period without bird strikes. One would expect the risk to be extremely low at night. However, statistics indicate that almost 15 per cent of the bird strikes occur at night.

In civil aviation, the risk of bird strikes is only in and around the aerodromes as that is the only time aircraft are operating at low heights within the common bird operating zones. In military aviation, this risk is present at areas other than aerodromes as military aviation by its very nature has to operate at low levels due to operational requirements. It is also necessitated at times by factors like weather, type of terrain, type of task and, of course, the operating limitations of the aircraft. Hence, military aircraft are more exposed to the risks of bird strikes. Our analysis shows that almost 50 per cent of bird strikes occur over the airfields while the balance 50 per cent occur off the airfields.

## History of Prevention

In the early years of aviation, bird strikes did not attract notice as the damage caused was less and generally did not result in loss of life and aircraft. The advent of jet engines brought the problem to the fore as the damage was unsustainable. Most airfields were away from populated areas, thus, remaining outside the human food chain. With rapid urbanisation and uncontrolled population growth, airfields are no longer safe havens but very much a part of the food chain sustaining bird activity

The early attempts at prevention were concentrated on avoiding populated / bird infested areas. With the advent of jets, and increased risk, even the flying hours began to be regulated based on common sense rather than any scientific method.

Slowly, the cost of aircraft escalated, and today is at astronomical figures. A modern fighter aircraft costs upwards of Rs 50 crore. The expenses involved in a bird strike accident forced the Air Force authorities to adopt a more professional approach. Extensive bird surveys of proposed low flying areas were conducted and only areas with low bird activity chosen. Regular bird surveys to monitor bird activity patterns were institutionalised. Simultaneously, the Bombay Natural History Society (BNHS) was given the task to survey 20 airfields and suggest measures to reduce bird activity over the bases.

## Chief Recommendations of BNHS

BNHS in its report stated that airfields are a lucrative habitat for birds where they find plenty of food. Deny them both the food and the habitat and they will go away. To achieve this, the methodology recommended was to remove all vegetation, shrubs and trees from the airfield area, keep grass limited to 6" to 8" height so that birds are not able to spot the insects and, hence, ignore the airfields.

For areas, surrounding the airfields the findings of BNHS stated that the major cause of bird hazard was the prevalent method of carcass disposal which utilises scavenger birds for carcass cleaning, and the open slaughter houses, open drains and open garbage dumps, in short, poor sanitation conditions. To improve the situation, they recommended that modern slaughter houses, incinerators and carcass processing centres be constructed, open drains be covered and open garbage dumps be shifted away from the airfields.

As can be visualised, implementing these measures requires a lot of capital outlay. But when the present cost of aircraft of around Rs 50 to 100 crore is compared to the capital outlay for implementing these measures, the money needed for it appears dwarfed and makes sound economic sense. Nevertheless, progress on these measures can be described, at best, as tardy.

## Types of Birds Involved

It will only be correct to devise preventive measures after understanding the types of birds and their operating heights. Birds in our environment that pose hazard can be classified into four categories:-

- Soaring birds.
- Medium / small birds
- Ground birds
- Migratory birds

### Soaring Birds

These are either scavengers like the vulture and pariah kite or predators like eagles and harriers. The greater danger, by far, is posed by the scavenger class, due to their large number, wide proliferation and high soaring ability – all dictated by the food chain. These birds can be encountered from ground level up to a height of 2 km, anywhere that aircraft operate. Being large, up to 4 to 5 kg in weight, they generally cause extensive damage.

### Medium / Small Birds

These are non-soaring birds that use the air space from ground level up to about 300 ft. They frequent wooded areas and scrub lands. They generally congregate near trees and shrubs which they use for perching, shelter, foraging and nesting. Examples of medium sized birds are the ubiquitous dove (white, ring necked or turtle), pigeon (blue rock), parakeet, mynah, egret and owl. These weigh 500 to 200 gm. Numerous smaller birds like the sparrow, starling, swallow and drongo are common. These weigh between 100 and 200 gm. All of these are found in large numbers at our airfields where food and habitat are in plentiful supply.

### Ground Birds

Peacocks, partridges, lapwing, etc form this family of ground birds. Other than the peacock, which weighs around 4 kg, these ground birds weigh from 100 to 400 gm. These pose a lesser hazard to aircraft, but hits by them are not uncommon.

### Migratory Birds

These are fairly large birds that also fly at great heights. Examples are the duck, goose and damoselle crane (kunj). Since these birds operate in large flocks and migrate seasonally, these are easily spotted and avoided. Being night fliers, they are sometimes struck during night flying. However, bird hit incidents with these birds are quite low.

## Bird Prevention Methods

As outlined in the statistics, bird hits on the airfield and off the airfield are occurring in roughly the same proportion. Therefore, the area to be targeted becomes extremely large. The types of birds that hit aircraft cover practically the whole spectrum of the bird population and the prevention programme, therefore, has to cover all the categories that have been described.

To make matters worse, birds are extremely intelligent and have great adaptability. If you are able to scare them today with one method, very soon the birds will recognise the method and will not be deterred by it. One has to then attempt another solution. In short, combating bird hazard has to be a continuous effort conforming to a dynamic model. Erecting a scarecrow may keep birds away for a short duration but soon the birds start perching on that very scarecrow. Farmers understand this and keep changing the shapes sizes clothes, look, etc of their scarecrows. One has no choice but to emulate this interactive dynamic method.

There are basically three ways of combating bird hazard.

- Eliminate birds.
- Scare away birds.
- Avoid birds.
- Awareness programme.

### Elimination of Birds

Elimination of birds through the direct method i.e. shooting, is not feasible, as the bird population is too large. However, through ecological means, their presence can be removed from the desired areas if one can ensure denial of food and shelter to them. This is no easy task but one that has to be undertaken. Destruction of nests and eggs on a regular basis can also lead to the reduction of birds in specific areas.

### Scaring the Birds

In this method, various types of bird scaring equipment in the audio as well as the visual spectrum is used. Gun shots, 12 bore cartridges, and pyrotechnics use a combination of audio and visual cues to scare birds away. Noise generators and ultrasonic equipment is also being experimented with. Some foreign firms have been toying with the idea of fitting the strobe light system to warn the birds of an impending collision. Most aircraft keep their landing lights on to warn the birds. Some even keep their radars on with the hope that these waves would warn the birds to move out of the path. In the USA, distress call tapes of birds are used to scare them away. In case the methodology is repeated continuously, the birds get used to it and the method loses its effectiveness.

### Avoiding Birds

The third method to combat the bird menace is to avoid birds during flying by deviating from their flight path. This can be done by forewarning the pilot about the area where bird activity is observed. With this knowledge, the pilot is able to deviate the aircraft from the bird infested areas. However, deviation is not possible during the take-off and landing phases as the aircraft is operating at its limits. The only answer then is to delay take-offs and landings to a more favourable time.

As IAF aircraft fly over large areas, this method would need a very extensive monitoring network in this vast stretch. It will also be manpower intensive. So the solution adopted is to position bird control teams over the airfield areas, and for local flying areas, carry out regular bird surveys. Based on the surveys, intensive bird activity areas are avoided and flying hours regulated to timings when bird activity is low.

### Awareness Programme

A major link in the bird control chain is to bring about awareness of this problem by educating the population that resides in and around the airfields of the causes of bird activity – availability of food and habitat – and the various methods available for combating it.

## IAF Bird Prevention Programme

Having seen the hazard posed by birds, the types of birds, and the methods available for reducing the bird menace, let us look at the bird prevention programme of the IAF.

The IAF has realised that there is no single answer to the problem of bird hazard. The strategy has to be multi-pronged and multi-layered as some of the action is at government level – both State and Centre. It has set up Bird Hazard Control Teams (BHCTs) at its bases, which not only report bird activity to the pilots but also take on the duties of scaring them / killing them.

Bird surveys of all local flying areas are undertaken and flying regulated to periods of low bird activity in areas which have less hazard of this type.

Scarecrows and mechanical scarecrows are a common sight at our airfields. Bird scaring through cartridges and pyrotechnics is practised. Imported noise generators, ultrasonics and strobe lights are at an experimental stage, and if found effective, will be established at all bases.

The IAF has realised that the ecological method of denying food and habitat to the birds is the best method. Therefore, the recommendations made by BNHS for combating the bird menace within the airfields are being implemented.

For measures outside the airfields involving sanitation in surrounding areas, the Ministry of Defence was able to obtain commitment of about Rs 10 crore from the Planning Commission in the Eighth Five-Year Plan. Currently, efforts are on by the Ministry of Defence to get a much larger funding for projects that involve sanitation measures around the airfields.

Educating the populace in and around the airfields on the causes of bird activity and the methods to combat it is done by the local station authorities with the help of village panchayats and audio-visual communications means available with them.

## Conclusion

It is seen that as bird strikes costs started escalating, the IAF embarked on a scientific plan to combat the bird menace. It realised that the threat came from soaring as well as non-soaring birds. As its area of operation is very wide, it had to evolve a strategy combining the three methods, i.e. elimination, scaring away, and avoiding birds. There can be no set answer to the problem of bird hazards as birds are intelligent and adapt themselves to changing scenarios fairly rapidly. In such a dynamic situation, the response too has to be ever changing and more dynamic. Moreover, the response has to be local for it is seen that what works at one place, may not work at another. In short, having bullied the birds out of their territorial rights, the IAF, like all big brothers, is now, trying to achieve peaceful coexistence with them. May it succeed. Amen. ❑

# Towards a Better Work Ethos

Over a period of time, executing routine chores and following orders is being seen as the fulfillment of the responsibility and accountability of an officer. In today's parlance, this is akin to a robotic response and certainly unacceptable.

The primary responsibility of the officer cadre is to guide and lead the Air Force so that it is always prepared to fight today's war, and is capable, both mentally and resources-wise, to forsee and absorb the changes in the nature of warfare as and when they come about. The responsibility of the officer cadre encompasses a host of required characteristics and different approaches. Professionalism is all encompassing and, in anything that we do, will always take pride of place. We must be professionals with high expertise levels. However, there are other aspects that also demand attention. I will concentrate on just three : training, forecasting and futuristic planning (planning for the future).

## Training

Training, in every facet and part of Air Force life, is an important and continuous need. Officers, SNCOs, airmen, cooks, gardeners, waiters, safaiwalas, etc. all need training and thereafter continued training to improve upon their craft. The need to train and the need to improve and become more efficient must become part of our mindset.

Training subordinates is a basic and major responsibility of an officer. The starting point must be the training of the officers themselves. While each individual is imparted basic training at training institutes, functionality is introduced at the station/unit level through continued training under more experienced people. Experience has taught us that even these experienced people have to be retrained regularly. Training and retraining have to be repeated and the officer must ensure that this is done on a continuous basis. The officer's involvement here will also improve his own knowledge/skill level. With emphasis on regular training and retraining, the skill levels will rise and, with the passage of time, less involvement of the officer may be needed, as the subordinates will be able to execute the assigned tasks with reduced supervision. Delegation will become a reality and the officer will be free to devote more time for his next responsibility – forecasting.

### Forecasting

Forecasting has many connotations but here I refer to the ability to visualise possible problem areas and contingencies that may crop up while executing the required tasks. With some practice and experience, the officer should be able to forecast problems and contingencies that could impede his functioning or attainment of his goals and objectives. A six monthly roll on forecast should be made every month, on a monthly basis if possible. Aircraft stagger, inspection schedules, effect of summer vacations with large leave percentages, effect of monsoons, shortage of spares, flying tasks, etc are some routine examples of areas that need to be considered whilst forecasting likely problem areas. Maintenance schedules of buildings, runways, etc also fall in the same category. The officer must utilise his experience, better knowledge base and skill to forecast trouble spots and thereafter formulate plans to ensure that the impact of the problems is greatly reduced if not obviated altogether. Thus, an officer who does good forecasting will be able to guide his subordinates in executing the tasks optimally as he will be mentally prepared to deal with possible roadblocks. Everyday "fire-fighting" will give way to "creating of fire lanes." The problem will reduce in intensity, permitting our officers time to try and improve our Air Force by effective planning.

### Futuristic Planning / Planning For The Future

Once again, the word "planning" has many connotations and nuances. In the present context, I use the word to encompass what we must think and do to make our Air Force better able to meet the tasks and the challenges it is likely to face.

Every officer should ask himself how he can improve his efficiency and contribute to the effectiveness of the Air Force, on the one hand, and the betterment of the Air Force, on the other. Some questions immediately come to mind : what are the innovations or changes needed to make my contribution more effective? Where should my squadron or unit or section be heading? What sort of goals and objectives should be set? How will we achieve them? How can the security and environment of the station be improved? How can the mindset of the subordinates be altered? What is the likely impact of technological advances on the prosecution of war that will impinge on the use of air power? What steps must be taken now to ensure that our Air Force remains modern and capable resource-wise, training-wise and thinking-wise? How can we enhance our operational effectiveness? How can we improve our productivity without increasing either manpower or material resources. There are many other issues that can and should come to mind. Answers must also be found and, wherever possible, implemented with dispatch. Futuristic planning alone can bring about the required improvement in our Air Force and, on time. It is the creative end of an officer's leadership function. Individually and collectively, our officer cadre must rise to the occasion and ensure that we are able to anticipate tomorrow's challenges and are good enough to combat them. ❑

# Interpersonal Relationships

Whenever improving interpersonal relationships is considered, holding PT, parades, social get-togethers, etc come to mind. Utilising the work place for it is generally not thought of. But, it is at the work place that the seeds of interpersonal relationship must be sown for lasting and enduring results.

The working place offers an abundance of opportunities for the officer to reach out to our personnel. When an officer chooses the work place for developing such relationships, a few spinoffs in supervision will also occur. An officer's regular presence at the work place, be it the orderly room, the store in logistics section, the tarmac or the hangar will lead to subordinates avoiding "wasting of time" and indulging in incorrect activities; his regular "presence" will automatically produce the desirable work culture. His visits and presence will offer him the opportunity to ensure that "unprofessionalism" or wrong practices are removed. It will provide an opportunity or a platform from where the subordinates could establish an informal link with the officer through the display of professionalism and then use this link for the betterment of the working environment or even ironing out personal problems. It will make the officer approachable. The methodology for using the work place for such interaction will depend on the individual and the local working environment, and would have to be worked out for each situation individually. What must be remembered is that there are very few individuals who are gifted by nature in creating bonds effortlessly. For most of us, these have to be developed deliberately and consciously.

Each individual desires to be a professional; more importantly, he likes to be seen as a professional. This desire, embedded in each one of us, regardless of rank, has to be nurtured and cultivated at the work place through regular interaction by officers. Emphasis on professionalism and greater interaction at the work place in an environment of openness and easier approachability is bound to produce a better work ethos. The social get-togethers, the welfare measures, the PT parades, essential as they are, will yield optimum results only when they are combined with such interaction at the work place. A word of caution. Whilst an officer must be approachable, he must never become familiar. His behaviour must be that of an officer, a leader and a gentleman at all times. He must ensure that his personal attributes, knowledge and professionalism are of a high order. Above all, he must be willing to learn and this willingness must be obvious and infectious.

Another area that demands our attention is the increased compartmentalisation that comes due to specialisation. Missile squadrons look differently at fighter squadrons who, in turn, look differently at transport / helicopter squadrons, etc. Similarly, radar units, different sections on a station *et al* have their own prejudices and personal opinions – some of which are neither accurate nor complimentary. Differences within the units / sections apart, differences abound within the branches and trades. All this happens due to a poor understanding of the other person's job and tasks. We must get over the feeling that only "I work" and all others do not. This can come about if conscious attempts are made at our stations to educate our personnel on each other's role, how it fits into the overall scheme, and its importance. Each individual has his part to play and none should seek to elevate his own role or downgrade another's. Visits to different sections / units and greater interaction should be encouraged and, if need be, formalised.

Each base would need to generate its own individual response to achieve a better work ethos, more professionalism, improved interpersonal relationship at work and a better understanding of what the other person's role is in the Air Force's scheme of things. ❑

# Annual Medical Examination Versus the Winged Warrior

There is this constant tension between a flyer and a doctor. The flyer perceives the doctor and his examination kit as an obstacle to be crossed, a sky to be conquered. May be the choice of labels itself has something to do with it. The terms "Annual Medical Examination" and "Medical Review Board" both contain words that reek of a test. And for the virile winged warrior, all tests have to be passed. By hook or by crook.

My first "close encounter" with the medical fraternity commenced rather early. At the NDA, the Air Force cadets had to undergo a medical exam in their fourth and sixth terms. In the fourth term, the Docs detected a DNS (deflected nasal symptom) in my nose. That I had a crooked nose, my mirror had informed me much earlier. It appeared that the Docs were keen to rectify God's design. An operation later, I learnt to my dismay, through the mirror again, that all the fancy scalpel work at the OT merely tweaked the issue internally and did absolutely nothing for the visuals. The Specialist Air Force Training was yet to commence. So this encounter with the Docs was perceived positively as it provided me with a few days of blissful rest at the hospital – away from the rigours of "physical education." The next encounter with the Docs was in the sixth term. By now, I had learnt about the Lift and the Drag and could even number Reynolds and was relishing the thoughts of flying. So when the eye specialist caught me for poor vision in the left eye (a partial 6/9 he said), I was taken aback. My course-mates straightaway pronounced that I would be in OG forever. I could not believe that my wings were clipped even before they could grow. A spiralling depression followed. A lot many visits and plenty of dilatory drops in the eyes later, my eyes were again declared a respectable 6/6 and my flying dreams resumed their colourful replay.

In those days, the basic stage of flying training was at Bidar and the intermediate stage was at Jodhpur after which the trifurcation took place. The fighter aspirants went to Hakimpet, the transport lot to Yelahanka and the helicopter boys remained at Jodhpur. Nearing trifurcation, the mood prevalent in the course was jubilant as the commission appeared at a graspable distance. Four years of gruelling training were behind us and only six months of the final stage separated us from the wings on the chest, the stripe on the shoulder and the head in the sky! Lo and behold! enters the Doc – the party spoiler – in the visage of a special medical for the fighter aspirants as they have to be "decompressed" prior to their jetting into the "high altitudes". Suddenly, the transport and helicopter boys became the focus of our envy as they would not be "tested", and their wings and rings would, thus, be safe. Some introspection later, the fear and envy subsides and the yet to be winged warrior brings out his claws. Must win this test – by hook or by crook. A SWOT analysis (never heard of in those days – management jargon was yet to surface) exposed the vulnerability in the eye region. A quick solution was readied – "mug up the vision test chart." In the good old days, Docs hadn't yet

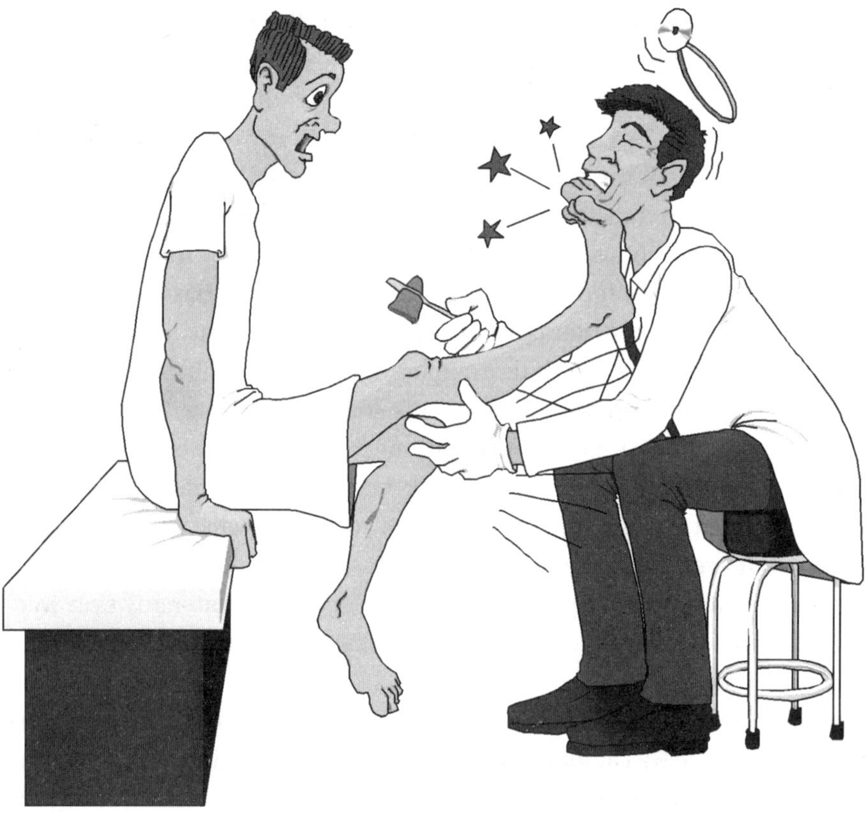

equipped themselves with the multiple charts which rotate at the flick of a button. In fact, to my pleasant surprise, the test was conducted by a helpful medical attendant who did not fuss about the exact distance between the eye and the chart. Less distance to conquer and a mugged up vision chart – a sure recipe for success. As it transpired, all this extra caution was highly unwarranted as I could actually read the chart with ease.

I did get my "wings and rings" on the appointed date. Yet the anxiety preceding and surrounding the actual examination brought forth one conclusion. Medical is a nuisance which cannot be avoided, but with some smart thinking and planning, can be neutralised. Docs are there to catch us and ground us. We have to avoid/trick them into letting us fly. So these medical exams then became a cat and mouse game.

The horror stories accompanying the "supersonic medical exam" in the late sixties and early seventies only furthered this impression, as apparently "fit" pilots were declared unfit to fly due to GTT indices which were later amended to suit Indian conditions. Was I alone in viewing medical exams with a suspicious eye? Definitely not. I merely reflected the popular opinion. Many a crew room session brought forth new tricks to deploy against the Docs. A trick that was awarded a perfect "10" by all was the urine test-tube trick. At the medical exam, you were handed over a test-tube and sent to a bathroom. You generally went with a friend. Each filled the test-tube with his urine sample and then exchanged the test-tube prior to handing over for the check. If one sample was found with traces of sugar, the owner would be called for a recheck. The recheck would be NAD (no abnormality detected) as the guy with the sugar was the person who has not been called for the recheck. So both escape with their "licence to fly" intact.

There is no doubt that flying is ecstasy and each pilot thinks that his wings have authorised him an unending joyride which no one should interrupt. Any person or procedure that comes in the way of this "joy" has to be neutralised. The doctor and the annual medical exam are thus seen to be spoilsports, party-killers, a pain, etc. Some of the doctors have only aided this perception by being non-sympathetic, bookish and officious. This whole gamut is, thus, seen negatively. With such an attitude, the correct perspective is lost. With age and experience, I have learnt that the correct way to view the annual medical exam is from the preventive and early detection/faster recovery angle. Let me illustrate. As COO Tezpur, many moons ago, the Docs caught me for high BP. Please note the words I have used. I said "caught me,"

implying entrapment for that is how we perceive it. Subsequent tests revealed that I was at the preliminary stage of a coronary tangle – what the Docs call the incipient stage. A quick "life-style change" (which I should have undergone as I turned 40) prompted by the station Docs and three months later, I cleared the Stress Thalium test. That led me back to my cockpit to pursue the unending joyride that I regarded as my birthright and destiny. You just have to look around and you will spot many fliers who were "put down" by the annual medical only to recover equally quickly as the process helped them to nip the problem at the bud stage itself. No doubt, the pessimists wearing the dark eyeshades will only spot the odd guy who was grounded by the Docs and then never got back to flying. The silver lining in this cloud is obviously ignored. That he is safe and living is not enough. What one is objecting to is the interruption to one's "birthright" of "unending joyride." I think we should change our perspective and our approach towards the medical exam. We should view it as an opportunity to detect "problems" at the incipient stage which helps us to obtain a solution in the shortest time-frame.

The wish of the winged warrior is to be airborne all the time. The "child" in him refuses to accept his physical ailments/shortcomings for the child is the greatest pursuer of joy and happiness. It is up to the "Adult Doc" to don a more positive attitude towards this "child" in the pilot and help him view this whole business of the medical exam more positively, more rationally. Is the onus only on the Docs? Yes and No. Yes, because it is their natural duty. Yes, because it is my close encounters with such Docs that has helped me transform my attitude towards the medical exam. No, because my wing-mates must also grow up and mature and change themselves. But then, don't you wish, you could remain a child always! Happy and innocent! Chasing simple pleasures! Like flying. So, Docs – help us grow up and convert the title of this article to "Annual Medical Exam AND The Winged Warriors," thus, replacing the "versus" with "and". ❑

# Quality Output From Op Inspectors

## Introduction

The Indian Air Force is seen today by the country as a vibrant modern force whose capability was acknowledged even by the Americans in the recent joint exercises. At the same time, its leadership wranglings, promotional policies, court cases have all marred its image, specially of senior officers, through continuous negative media exposure. Internally, the personnel too view the Service with misgivings as they find that there is inconsistency in its human resource policies. It is felt that the most valuable asset of the Air Force, namely, its personnel, are not managed well. This paper attempts to provide a methodology for recasting its human resources policies in a more scientific manner using the available software tools and the highly motivated professionals available with the ACAS (I). It also suggests a few redefined roles for these experts which will improve our operational capabilities.

## History of DASI

During the 1971 war, one of the major lessons learnt by the IAF was that its air bases lacked a lot of the standard facilities and infrastructure so necessary for operations. This led to the formation of the Directorate of Air Staff Inspection (DASI). DASI inspected bases, produced reports on levels of operation preparedness and pointed out deficiencies in op 'infrastructure' training, etc. DASI reports were given phenomenal weightage and the deficiencies pointed out were corrected on 'fast track'. Over the decades, basic minimum operation and maintenance facilities were created and DASI then did not have any major deficiencies to point out. DASI reports no longer created any waves and DASI visits did not produce any tremors.

DASI tried to expand its scope of inspection to include Command HQ. This, however, led to the resignation of an IG. Recently, DASI has changed its tack and "visited" two Command HQ for "interaction". The aim of this interaction is restricted to studying the op plans as this would enable DASI to understand the field interpretation of their execution when they inspect the wings and squadrons.

It is clear from the above that the DASI charter needed a change a long time ago but this was not done. Close to 48 officers with DASI, DMI and DAI (2 Air Commodores, 3 Gp Capts and 43 Wg Cdrs – all exceptional professionals) have been utilised for a large number of years as merely "quality inspectors". It is time this lot of professionals under ACAS (I) was used for some "quality output."

### Quality Output from Op Inspectors

Having established that there are many quality professionals under ACAS (I) who can be tapped for much more quality output, this paper sets forth the methodology for it. This has been done in two parts.

- **Part I - Human Resources Management: The Problem Area.** In this part, the problem area is identified and a suitable solution suggested.
- **Part II - Enhancing Operational Effectiveness.** A few simple easily implementable suggestions are put forward. If implemented, these would enhance the operational effectiveness manifold.

## PART I: HUMAN RESOURCES MANAGEMENT

### Problem Areas

#### Movers and Shakers

All organisations are driven by a small percentage of people. This is true for the IAF also. Regardless of the marks in P 57, it is a reality that a majority of the members in the IAF are just average. The better of these, through selection, get promoted to higher ranks. There is elimination at each select rank. This provides the famous "pyramid" shape to our hierarchy. Are all those who get promoted equal in their output? It cannot be. Only some of them will be entitled to the honour of being termed as "the movers and the shakers". At each rank, there will be some key appointments that should or must be filled with these "movers and shakers"? One can safely conjecture that the number of such personnel will generally be lower than the slots needing them. This figure would vary each year for each rank, as different courses come up and the seniors slip off the pyramid into retirement/release. Let us assume that we have fewer "movers and shakers" but more slots needing them. Producing more "movers and shakers" is not possible as this is not a factory product. So what should be done? Someone who understands what the Air Force is all about has to sit down and then prioritise these slots so that at least the more important ones always get the better people. This is not to suggest that there are no QRs for slots, or that postings are made in an ad hoc manner. What is missing is an overall view/knowledge/assessment of the quality numbers, a prioritisation of the important slots and a well considered scientific method for filling them. With such analysis and prioritisation, "P" staff would know which are the areas that are not getting the leadership they deserve. Knowledge of weak areas would help in producing a mechanism to ensure that these do not become critical. As the number of movers and shakers will vary from year to year, a dynamic model would need to be evolved.

**Key Portfolios for Operational Success**

Has anyone done any homework to understand which are the key portfolios in the IAF that, if filled correctly, would define success for the IAF, as these are the pillars of the IAF's operational success? We have to look after our officers – however, the right officer should be placed at the right job. We should not sacrifice our operational efficiency at the altar of looking after the individual's career prospects.

**Importance of 'Int'!**

The intelligence agencies need Air Force officers to help them sift out relevant "info bytes" for Air Operations from the massive data that is collected by them. Such slots should be recognised as key appointments and must be manned, and manned well, for operational success.

**Specialisation vs Tenures**

To specialise on any system, one needs longer tenures but then this would bring it into conflict with the turnover policy; and equal geographical opportunity for all. Do we favour the individual or the system or accept a sub-optimal solution, with maximum interest groups losing out? It is no secret that to become an *Ustad* on any type of aircraft, airmen/technical officers have to get a lot of experience on maintenance work on the same type. How do we marry this truism with our policy based on tenures? Should we lose out on *Ustads* because they must be posted out east to complete their east tenure? Or some individuals must remain continuously in the east as they are *Ustad* on a type available only in the east? Has any mathematical modelling been done to see the various combinations, the needs of the organisation, the numbers available, the choices possible, etc? Have we worked out various combinations mathematically and seen what effect each will produce? Are our policies based on well-researched info bytes or just hunches or reactions of the individual in the chair? By and large, we react to situations as they crop up and produce a "generally satisfying solution." Should we not aim to be more scientific and in this "smart age" produce a SMART solution that is higher in satisfaction levels? Again, the model produced has to be dynamic to accommodate ever changing needs and situations.

**Career Planning**

What should a career planning graph look like for each branch? Should it change regularly or not change at all? Does it look after the aspirations of our large force at the expense of operational efficiency or vice versa? Should AE (L) officers focus on radars or communication? Should EW experts stay in EW? Should fliers keep changing their fleet? What is an optimum amount of flying experience an any type? Should some pilots keep enjoying the high end technology aircraft and others be relegated to only MiG-21s? Should we increase the quota for Short Service Commissioned Officers? Would the motivational levels of our personnel be better served with more "Branch Commissions"? There are a million such questions which all need logical human resource answers. No solution will satisfy all. But application of scientific tools to the problems is likely to produce a more satisfying solution.

**Courses**

The Service offers a variety of courses. A few are termed career courses and these are well sought after. Others pose a manning problem. In this knowledge driven era, courses are a must. This is common knowledge, yet "P" staff finds it extremely difficult to fill these slots while the field commanders have extreme difficulty in releasing individuals for them. Shortage of manpower is a known fact. But has anyone done any analysis to see if some courses can be scrapped/reduced in a time-frame/replaced by distant learning methodology? Short absences from units due to courses become acceptable to the field formations whereas lengthy absences pose problems. Courses definitely need a review.

**Promotion Policies**

I have only touched the tip of the iceberg and raised a few issues. I have purposely kept promotions and the policies surrounding them out of this paper. But these too represent a large segment of "P" staff work that comes under the scanner daily in the field, and every now and then in the Press.

## The Solution

**Revised Manning Architecture of the IAF: Methodology**

So how does one solve this critical Human Resource Problem of the Air Force? A committee of good dedicated professionals must be set up, with a fixed time-frame for its output. It must go to all kinds of field units in all geographical areas. It must interact with the vast majority of people and obtain from them the kind of "P" issues that bother them. This must cut across all branch/rank structures. Having understood what bothers the lower portion of our personnel pyramid, it must then interact with the management functionaries at the field level, Command Headquarters and various Branches and their Directorates at Air Headquarters to understand the organisational viewpoints and why some decisions were made. After this, the team must interact with "P" staff/AFRO staff. At this stage, the existing policies must now be matched with the inputs received from the field and higher formations. This matching will obviously result in surfacing of problems, shortages, demands, etc. This is the stage where problems will get defined and quantified. Now this team must use mathematical modelling, computers, our famous software/skills, and produce a manning architecture of the IAF and HR policies. It must also review the courses conducted, their time-frames and vacancies, and recommend which can be replaced with distant learning. Who should be in this team? This is where the large pool of quality professionals (48 at the last count) from DASI, DMI and DAI would come in. Place a large number of them, with the ACAS (PO) as the chairman. The biggest advantage of using DASI personnel for such a task is that they are supposed to understand our operational philosophy best and, hence, would hopefully ensure that the "P" policies of the IAF serve it best operationally. They are also the most suitable professionals who can identify the slots that need movers and shakers as well as the key portfolios for operational success.

**Mathematical Modelling**

The major emphasis in this tasking is the use of scientific tools by this committee. Software available in the market for HR must be exploited. Mathematical modelling must be utilised copiously to find the appropriate solution.

**Holistic View**

Is there an accusing finger pointing towards the AOP's branch in all these assertations? At first glance, that could be the surmise. But that is definitely not the intention. Of course, "P" staff/AFRO react to all the suggestions/problems as they crop up. But a holistic view, on the lines suggested above, has probably not been taken. We need to be proactive and not reactive. If all the facets are seen together, the problems identified after interaction with all involved, and solutions produced scientifically, using modern software tools and expert professionals, the personnel architecture and policies that would surface would definitely enhance motivation, productivity and efficiency.

**Reaction to "Reforms Committee"**

Once this reforms committee is formed and interacts with the field, the reaction from the "personnel pyramid" would be extremely positive, for each member of the IAF would realise that there is somebody up there who "cares" for them and wants to address all the personnel issues faced by them. This itself will wipe out the negative vibrations in the atmosphere and serve as a motivator. The leadership will once again be viewed in a positive light.

## PART II : ENHANCING OPERATIONAL EFFECTIVENESS

This part provides four implementable suggestions for enhancing our operational effectiveness. It suggests creation of "Lessons Learnt Teams" which function somewhat like umpires in our exercises, to create packages for E-learning now that our networks are ready/close to ready, getting grassroots involvement in op planning and about modifying op inspections and their format. The link throughout these suggestions is the quality manpower available with ACAS (I).

## Lessons Learnt Teams

### Current Umpiring Methodology

In our methodology of operations, mid-course corrections/refinements to our op plans, etc take place only when the results pour in, in the form of mission reports/debriefs or if some events occur that force us to rethink the way we are executing the operations. In peace-time exercises, our methodology for learning lessons relies on the umpires. These are experts loaned out by the Commands not participating in the exercise. The umpires jot down all the shortcomings they have seen during the exercise and then these are presented to the commander by the chief umpire at the end of the exercise as debrief. In this method, corrections from the lessons can be applied only at the next Command exercise

### The US Methodology

The US forces have evolved a different methodology for learning lessons. Both in Afghanistan and the recent Iraq campaign, they employed "Lessons Learnt Teams." A set of experts was assigned to field formations. These teams/experts report back to the commander on a daily basis on how the field commanders perceived the orders and how they were executed. This is in addition to the standard mission reports/debriefs. As the report cycle/duration was 24 hours, the commander was able to know immediately if his op plan was perceived as he intended and got a neutral observer's opinion on its execution. He could then set in motion a correction mechanism, if felt necessary. Such a methodology was found to be extremely beneficial as it compressed the time-frames and allowed the commanders an ability to finetune/correct their op plans as they were unfolding.

### Expertise Available with DASI

DASI possesses these military experts and the manpower needed for the "Lessons Learnt Teams." DASI, DMI and DAI members should be used for all Command exercises as umpires with the time cycle of 24 hours for the feedback loop. This will ensure that the lessons are learnt by the planners and the executers immediately and not relegated for the next exercise/war. In the past, Command HQs have attempted to obtain DASI members as umpires for their exercises but the organisational turfs and the perceived importance to the act of "Op Inspections" did not allow them to be used in this role. Again, the benefits of using the DASI personnel for such a task is immense as they are supposed to understand our operational philosophy best. The same set of experts used by different Commands would also result in cross-pollination as well as standardisation in our operational philosophy.

## E-Learning

### Networks and Education

The pilots today are extremely conscious of the fact that they have to be continuously on a learning curve. With computers and the internet, information available has exploded to gigantic proportions. The need of the hour is to select the relevant bytes and package it for learning by our young flying fraternity so that they can push their professional boundaries. Projects for connectivity at field and HQ level in the form of LAN and WAN are underway in a big way. Some geographical regions are already interlinked. In each such case, the focus of connectivity is primarily organisational. These networks would have vast capability of info storage and info flow. This spare capacity and networking must be used to enhance the knowledge levels of our professionals. How do we do this?

### Knowledge Domain with ACAS (I)

ACAS (I) has the necessary experts with him in AEB, DASI, DMI and DAI. A group under CO AEB with DASI members could be tasked to produce e-learning packages for our pilots. These could be loaded on the WAN/LAN. A DMI team could be tasked to use Tetra and other available packages and come up with suitable material that could be used by our technicians/engineers/pilots for their knowledge/skill enhancement, at the field level. DAI could produce a similar package for the non-technical branches. For this task, a fixed time-frame must be given to the group and the results put to use by the people already networked. It could be improved after user feedback so that the final version is ready by the time our elaborate network plans get established on the ground fully.

## Operational Planning for the Next War

### Grassroots Involvement in Op Planning

Kargil and Op Parakaram left behind a large number of lessons. Since then, a variety of force multipliers and hi-tech aircraft/weaponry has been inducted or is in the pipeline. At the same time, a lot of war machinery has been numberplated. Manpower shortages abound. Have we taken these new realities on the ground and included them into our op plans? Have we taken an overview of our new capabilities and dovetailed them into our tactics and strategies? Of course, the relevant Commands and various Directorates at Air HQs have their views on the subject, and their respective plans have been modified to cater for each of these new elements. There is, however, a need for wider discussions on the issues involved. Today's youngsters are professionals whose views must be heard. Discussion/op seminars must be encouraged on these subjects. The IG branch is the most suitable agency for their conduct. The ideas generated must then be evaluated and if found, fit tested in a mini-exercise by Command HQs wherein DASI must also be involved in planning, execution and umpiring. This would have to be followed by laying down the methodology for training for these op events by suitable inclusion in the Annual Squadron Training/Exercises specially designed for such training. Once the new operational philosophy gets embedded into our flying training, we will not be fighting the next war with yesterday's tactics.

## Modified Inspection Format

### CASI Visits: Modified Format

In the military, inspections are a must for they act as auditors of our sense of responsibility and ensure that we are not found wanting in the time of war. But for DASI inspections, a lot of things would not get done. So can we afford to stop DASI inspections? We should not stop inspections but we can definitely modify the methodology. As explained earlier, a very high level of professionals in DASI are executing a routine defined task. This must change. DASI inspections must be left to Command HQ and their CASI teams. The format of CASI inspection would need to be recast with the help of DASI. The time cycle would also need to be revised. The Command Op Staff do not possess the quality in numbers that DASI possesses. Therefore, the new CASI format would have to accommodate this reality in its revised inspection schedule. In any case, the goal of DASI inspection was to assess whether a unit is fit/prepared for its operational tasks. This goal does not need the expertise of DASI. As far as operational preparedness is concerned, each Command HQ takes stock of its potential and preparedness in its annual exercise. If the suggestions given in this paper are accepted, then the presence of DASI as umpires in these exercises will enable both Air HQs and Command HQs to get feedback on operational readiness/preparedness.

**Revision of DASI Charter**

If DASI is not utilised for routine inspections of field units, what should be its charter? Should its composition change? Should it remain rich with such high quality professionals or should it be made leaner? Some of the tasks suggested in this paper are one-time special tasks, while some are of a regular nature. It is suggested that till these one-time tasks are completed, DASI strength should be maintained at this level. The DASI charter should be modified and its inspection effort shifted upwards to include Command HQs. The Command op plans must be brought under its purview. The focus of its inspection must shift from individual commanders and field formations to organisational/system deficiencies which degrade operational preparedness. In conjunction with Command HQs, percentage surprise inspections of field formations must be done.

## Conclusion

It was seen that for the past few years, the valuable quality professionals available with ACAS (I) were being utilised for a routine task, with an output not commensurate with the quality of the personnel involved. It was felt that much more valuable quality output could be obtained from these professionals. A major area where they could contribute was in refashioning/utilisation of the human resource architecture of the IAF and the associated policies. Their professional knowledge base, coupled with the modern scientific tools available in the market, could produce solutions which would lead to enhanced motivation of our personnel, better productivity and enhanced efficiency.

These same professionals could also be utilised for increasing our operational potential. Formation of "Lessons Learnt Teams" producing packages for e-learning, broader discussion on utilisation of our force multipliers and modifying our inspection charter and format have also been suggested. Implementation of these suggestions would definitely enhance our operational potential and ensure that we do not fight the next war with yesterday's tactics. ❑

# New Year Resolution

The grand success story of the seventies was the moon landing of Neil Armstrong. Its foundation was laid by President Kennedy when he endorsed the aim of the American space programme as landing a man on the moon. There is lesson in it for all of us. Aim high and persevere. Success will be yours.

Suppose our Air Force was to aim for Zero Accidents! Impossible! Unachievable! Unrealistic! Such will be the response echoing from the pavilion. Realistically speaking, such a response would be considered appropriate by the vast majority. I, too, would have responded in the same vein till I came across the following set of statistics in one of the issues of *Combat Edge* – a USAF safety magazine. Quote:

Without a goal of zero, we would have to accept the following:

- 2 unsafe landings per day at the Academy.
- 16,000 pieces of mail lost every hour by the postal services.
- 20,000 incorrect drug prescriptions per year.
- 500 incorrect surgical operations each week.
- 50 new-born babies dropped at birth daily by doctors.
- 22,000 cheques deducted from the wrong bank accounts each hour.
- Nine misspelled words on every page of a magazine.

Suddenly, the goal of zero accidents makes a lot of sense. Unquote.

Do you still think this goal is unachievable? How will you know unless you try, and try real hard, to achieve it? The best way to do it is to establish a personal goal of zero accidents. May be, like the plague, this virus of zero accidents will spread. So let this be your New Year Resolution. ❑

# Quality Audit

**(Extracts from Keynote address – IFSCON-2007)**

Operational capability depends on good training. A sound training programme implies that the *margins of the man and the machine are so defined that operations are done within this envelope, with adequate cushioning effect available for contingencies*. Thus, *training would cater to envisaged operational scenarios as well*. Again, we see that flight safety and operational capability are synchronous to each other. The problem lies in the *miscomprehension of what is expected from our warriors by our warriors in times of combat operations*. Take the case of Operation Desert Storm. During the preparations for the war, a few accidents in the air power of the coalition forces took place in the sands of the Arabian desert. This was a matter of concern for the air commander because his prime focus had been on preserving his assets during the preparatory stage. During investigations, it was discovered that the actual reason for most of the accidents was that the *crew were training too hard, pushing their aircraft, flouting rules and following tactics that were too risky for the situation*.

When pilots deploy in such situations, the constraints are lessened. And *when they deploy in anticipation of war, the lure to go beyond the limits seems falsely justified to them. As a result, they often exceed their own capabilities* and create situations that saturate their capacity to cope; they put their aircraft in positions that defy the laws of physics, and are unable to recover. Thus, one can see that it is the human factor, more than anything else, that results in losses, be it training in peace or in war. *Operations without safety would not only be hazardous but would erode the nation's credibility as a deterrent potent force in quick time*. Thus, flight safety and operational capability remain interwoven and complementary to each other. *No real conflict ever results from their integral functioning*. It is up to us to bring this awareness at all levels in our organisations and do away the wrong notions, if any, about flight safety hindering operational capability.

So, where do we go from here and what does the future hold for us? The future lies in giving "quality" the highest priority. What do we mean by quality? To begin with, let us look at what constitutes military aviation. We hold vast assets of material and equipment that contribute immensely to our effective operational capability. Therefore, we need to ensure that quality remains the driving force for this inventory of ours. Failure of quality in any aspect in our inventory could lead to disastrous consequences. Remember the last flight of the Concorde which resulted in a catastrophe? And what was the investigation result? A component of another aircraft had fallen off on the runway after take-off. While the Concorde was taking off, this piece of material ricocheted off the wheels and pierced the undercarriage section, leading to an uncontrolled chain of events terminating in a catastrophe. It is obvious that quality was missing here. Does this not drive home the point on the impact of poor quality? Is it not absolutely necessary to make quality an integral and foolproof part of our functioning? Thus, we need to have top-of-the-class quality in every stage of our inventory.

Vivid images of the Pyramids of Egypt, the Lighthouse of Alexandria or the Taj Mahal in India, overwhelm us in awe. They stand in mute testimony to the immense capability of our species. Conceived with brilliance, constructed with uncanny passion and fructified with the continued perseverance of generations, these monuments are edifices of quality conception, quality work and quality product through an interwoven quality process. Therefore, we too should pick the lesson of "Quality Consciousness" from these beautiful "Wonders of the World" and apply this quality consciousness to all our endeavours.

All our materials and inventories are governed by processes and procedural aspects. Naturally, the next step is to ensure that quality is instituted as the *mantra* for the "processes" in our systems. Today, we have various tools like Six Sigma, SAE AS 9100 and various models like the KAIZEN to ensure that our processes reach a standard of high quality. Once quality is ensured, the natural by-product would be enhanced and effective flight safety. Therefore, we need to set "chasing quality" as a goalpost for ourselves.

We also need to ensure that the interface between the materials and the processes too must be quality oriented. Although the materials and the processes, as independent identities, may be quality oriented, we need to ensure that the multitude interfaces wherein they are expected to 'talk' to each other too are made quality oriented. We have been witness to so many accidents in the past when this interface had failed despite the individual entities being quality oriented. We have had accidents when avionics of aircraft were not compatible with the runway aids or cases wherein avionics in different aircraft were not compatible, resulting in near-misses, or different procedures followed by military and civil aviation, leading to hazardous situations when they operate together. Thus, ensuring a foolproof and quality interface assumes paramount importance.

Chasing quality is expensive. Quality costs money, but that's only to be expected if one needs to have a potent and combat-worthy force that is ever ready to be applied. We are all affected by environmental changes, changing geo-political situations, tight budgetary controls, amongst other things, which entail cutting down on expenditure. But then, each accident also involves colossal costs and adversely affects our war-waging potential itself. The price our organisation will have to pay in achieving quality in terms of manpower, checks, processing, equipment, etc., though not small, will reap rich dividends that will be immense and of much significance. Therefore, we need to focus on the vision for the future viz. start the marathon chase for quality and relentlessly pursue it. Thus, quality in the years to come would form a major pillar in the realm of flight safety.

In today's scenario, aircraft losses all around the world mostly result from human and technical failures. Technology has a direct bearing on the number of accidents due to technical failures. Analyses over the years have driven home the point very strongly that vintage technology has contributed significantly to aircraft losses. We in the IAF too have had to resort to various measures to neutralise the effect of old technology on our flight safety record. In the last few years, we have brought down the number of losses due to technical failures primarily by measures like phasing out older technology, increased interaction with the OEMs, review of maintenance practices, conducting periodic quality audits, etc. Technology today also enables us to ascertain design deficiency and locate flaws at the manufacturing level, thereby, reducing the potential dangers. We are confident that with better technology being inducted into the IAF in the near future, these losses would further reduce.

What remains a problem for the IAF, remains as well a problem for the Air Forces around the world, and that is, losses due to human failures continue to remain more or less at a steady but unacceptably high percentage. Over the years, this figure has not changed much. Although the reasons for human failures may differ from country to country, by and large, the overall percentage contribution of human failures resulting in aircraft losses has remained constant for all nations. This remains a cause of worry for all of us. What I perceive is that with the improved technology being inducted, there will be an overall reduction in the losses of aircraft. Thus, the bubble of aircraft losses will gradually shrink. But, despite the shrinking bubble, the contribution of human failures in losses will still remain substantially high. Reducing the human failures will be the biggest challenge for all the Air Forces around the world. I envisage that the focus of flight safety programmes will shift towards managing human factors in aviation and finding a solution by understanding the complexities and limitations of the human being.

The effectiveness of the man/machine/environment decides the operational capability of any Air Force. Of the three, the man remains most vulnerable due to inherent physiological limitations of our species since nature did not design us to take to the air. A lot of effort has gone into enhancing the human capabilities to defy nature's laws and enable man to aviate. With advancing technology, the machines are capable of taking stress that is well beyond the human capacity. We have also put in a lot of effort in ensuring that the man in the cockpit is made more tensile, thereby, attempting to reduce the disparity in capability between him and the machine. Thus, the F-16 has been designed with a reclined seat, along with an unconventional joystick; mechanisms for increased "g" tolerances have been evolved and simulators have been created for training in these aspects. The efforts are still continuing.

With technology, we would be able to stretch the man physiologically and train him better through simulators and other tools, but the problem of understanding the psychological issues in the man remain a challenge. We would need to understand human capability, its response, its limitations, and the limits to which a person can be stretched as also to learn to recognise signs of failure. The task at hand is far more intricate and complex than is apparent. The right combination of Man, Machine and Environment, under the right circumstances, would remain a potent and lethal force to reckon with. Yet, at the same time, the combination can be fraught with vulnerabilities due to the involvement of a human element in it – so vital an ingredient yet so unpredictable. Why do some pilots get disoriented in routine missions while some under similar situations don't?

Why do some get stressed while some do not get stressed at all? Why do some pilots give adequate indications of impending human failure while others do not display an iota of symptoms despite the problem existing? A fighter pilot is an aggressive combat warrior, trained to strike the lethal blow and accomplish his mission aim. And we tell him, "Son, don't push yourself too hard and stick to your limits." Will he? Do we really understand the psyche of this being? Or do we want fighter pilots to be a different breed of combat pilots in the future? Would they be more of combat managers than combatants themselves in the wars to come? And even then, would the change of role make them invulnerable to the travails today's combat pilot goes through? Would technology offer us solutions for looking into the human mind and deciphering ways and means of determining his limits? And would we be able to control the changing dynamics and environment that could overwhelm our warriors? The answers to most questions would emerge in the future.

To conclude, I would like to say that since the days of the Wright brothers, aviation has come a long way to reach the present state we are in today. Our Air Forces have evolved through a constant process of adaptation to the demands of the changing world. Starting with indiscriminate use, air power suffered excessive losses in World War I and World War II. Only then did we realise that air power and its application needed to be planned meticulously so as to preserve it too. With the induction of expensive technology and lethal capabilities, no longer could we afford to fritter away our precious resources. This is where flight safety made its presence felt, not by inhibiting, but by embedding itself in the conduct of operations so that we became more effective in application, yet also preserved our assets. Thus, one can say that a balance between operational capability and flight safety was achieved by the time the millennium had turned. Today, we face newer challenges. Technology continues its giant strides into the future. The Man/Machine/Environment combination remains all-important, yet only quality at all levels can guarantee safety. Quality in thinking, quality in materials and equipment and quality in processes can ensure that we remain on the track of safe aviation. Therefore, quality in the way we do things will be the driving factor if we want to keep our air power soaring safely.

Despite the fast-track evolution of aviation and despite the overwhelming effects of technology in all activities, we still have not been able to detach the human being from being the brain behind the machine.

Man continues to occupy the critical post of a "decision-maker" in the air power scenario. Unfortunately, man has not been designed to endure the stretched limits that technology otherwise enables us to. With the help of technological advances, we may have been able to alleviate the problems to some extent. On the psychological level, the challenge lies in finding solutions to the barrier that psychological aspects in a human being present to us. Finding an answer to problems like disorientation, stress, fatigue, etc. will be the roadmap for us in the future. Therefore, it is up to us as guardians of our resources and combatants, to ensure that our organisation is moulded to generate a qualitative approach and, focus on the psychological aspects of piloting. These will assure that we are able to preserve our precious resources. ❑

## SECTION – IV

# BEYOND FLIGHT: THE CYBER SPACE

# Disinformation and Media Management

## Introduction

The First War of Independence fought in 1857, which was termed by the British as the "Sepoy Mutiny," was triggered by a rumour that the British were coating rifle cartridges in animal fat. Contact with this fat was taboo to both the Hindu and Muslim soldiers. This "belief" spread like wildfire and resulted in a tremendous uprising against the British.

The *Mahabharata* records an incident in which the news that "Ashwathama" had been killed was disseminated. "Ashwathama" was the name of a famed elephant as well as the name of Dronacharya's heroic son. The elephant was killed but the news carefully hid this fact and only highlighted the name. The intended aim of this disinformation was to increase the vulnerability of master warrior Dronacharya. To lend authenticity to this piece of half-truth, an affirmation was obtained from the fountain of truthfulness, Yudishtra, who confirmed that Ashwathama had indeed died. Yudishtra took refuge in the technicality that he was referring to the famed elephant. The desired result was obtained.

In World War II, the landing site of Normandy for the Allied invasion was camouflaged by phenomenal deception measures to lead the Nazis to believe that the attacks would come at another site. In the Gulf War, the Americans too managed to deceive the Iraqi forces about the direction of attack. All these were performed through a meticulous disinformation campaign executed through various media available at that time.

## Aim

The aim of this paper is to study the applicability of disinformation and propaganda as weapons of war today and the consequent media management.

## Art of Propaganda and Disinformation

Propaganda must be based on information which, to the enemy, is credible. Therefore, it must have good research and intelligence at its base. It must stem from a deep understanding of the target audience and must get the right message to the right audience at the right time. It should be presented in a form which will both attract and excite, while exploiting the target's physiological and psychological needs which it should then seek to satisfy. It should be neither excessively rigid nor dogmatic, nor unnecessarily hostile or contentious. It must therefore, necessarily be selective.[1]

The most important attribute of Disinformation and Propaganda is that both must be credible i.e. believable. Help here can be taken both from fact and fiction. The aim is to lure the receiver into believing something that would further one's cause. Audiences are more likely to accept an idea if they believe it was heard inadvertently i.e. in the style of "matter of fact." A message presented in an assertive way will be resisted. Opinions can be changed if a message is received from a variety of sources that mutually reinforce each other. People tend to approve of statements made by experts or by those who begin by expressing an opinion with which the listener or viewer strongly agrees. Under some circumstances, propaganda messages can be made more potent by incorporating opposing arguments in a way that tends to discredit them. The audience gets the impression that it is viewing both sides of the story.

Disinformation and propaganda can both be classed as non-lethal weapons of war. They are certainly not the product of modern technology and have a history dating back to mythologies. Today's vocabulary, however, does have a classification, "non-lethal weapons," that can describe them accurately. Their usage, in both war and peace, to further one's cause is extremely well known and documented.

## Social Contract

Throughout history, war has been central to the emergence, conduct and survival of the state in all its forms, from the tribe to the modern nation-state. In turn, the origins of the state rest on the social contract, whereby men and women gathered together and subordinated their individual rights in order to gain a common defence of life and property and the other benefits that flowed from cooperation and association. However, no matter

1. Mark Llyod, *The Art of Military Deception*, Book Mart Publishers, New Delhi, 2001, p.139.

what political organisation emerged, everything revolved around the tacit bargain of consent and the voluntary abrogation of rights on the part of the individual and the community in support of the common good, with defence as the most pressing issue.

From these early times, the first demand on a monarch or a leader under the social contract was to protect the peace, to repel invasion, and to wage war in the interests of the group. Without exception, it was accepted that the ruler had the right to command the citizen's duty of obedience in time of war.

This social contract has been valid throughout history. It was reinforced in World War II, where the threat of death and destruction was shared equally by the civilians and frontline soldiers. In the case of democracies, the populations readily accepted the abrogation of their rights, including that of a free Press.[2] At times, this social contract wears the garb of patriotism and exacts the same penalties from the population. President Bush successfully misled his nation into believing that Iraq was in nexus with the terrorists and possessed a stockpile of weapons of mass destruction. The US Senate, Congress and, in fact, the whole nation supported him when he invaded Iraq. Social contract continues to be valid and relevant.

Even in independent India, social contract has been valid throughout. In our conflict with China and Pakistan, the Indian public has wholeheartedly supported the government. In fact, these hostilities gave rise to huge waves of patriotism and willingness on the part of everyone to help the military achieve its aim.

## Media Management

Initially, it was easy for the state and the military to manipulate the media so that the public opinion supported the war aims. But once the reporter reached the battlefront and possessed the means to communicate, the equation began to change.

The capability of the military and the state to manipulate public opinion weakened. The fact that the media could present views other than the war aims of the military was anathema to the military. As a result, censorship, or at least the limitation of information, rapidly became the norm during war. This was rationalised as a requirement of the "operational security" of the troops involved.[3] To a certain degree, this was true. However, more often

2. Peter Young and Peter Jesser, *The Media and the Military*, London, 1997, pp.6-8.
3. Ibid., p.25.

than not, the military used its powers to extend the fog of war. It used its powers to colour the information to its war aims and then release it. It used the "social contract" and "patriotism" to obtain control over the media. Both the World Wars saw this. The Press and radio were manipulated by both sides to further their military aims. Germany was quite open about media manipulation whereas the Allies did it discreetly.

In the case of India, right upto the Indo-Pak conflict of 1971, mainly the Press and radio were around as media. Radio was a government monopoly which faithfully mouthed the official version. The Press too accepted every official bit as fact and reported it as such. The massive wave of patriotism that accompanied each conflict also did not allow the Press to seek or think of independent reporting as the unwritten social contract overshadowed such notions. The opportunity to "manage the media" existed, but the Indian military did not use it.

### Limited Wars and "Independent Media"

After World War II, the nature of warfare has been changing and has given rise to a wide variety of warforms – the most prominent of these is the limited conflict or low intensity conflict. The "limited" nature of the "lower" intensity often ensures that only a segment of the population of the nation is threatened or involved, leaving the vast majority sort of "uninvolved". At times, the conflict is conducted a large distance away from the "nations." Such attributes ensure that total unqualified backing by the public is not obtained and, in fact, the very "justness" of the conflict begins to be questioned.[4] In such cases, the mass media do not abrogate their rights and, instead, insist on their fundamental duty to inform the public. The Vietnam War was a classic example of the situation where the "social contract" between the citizens and the government was questioned. The media became a free and independent player, with the capacity to influence both the conduct of hostilities, and particularly through its impact on popular sentiment, the direction of government policy. In fact, such was the sway of the public opinion that the US government was finally forced to negotiate peace and withdraw. In the Vietnam War, the role of the media and its interaction with the military was an exception. Citizens and the media, by and large, continue to stay within the bounds of the social contract, support the conflict and willingly abrogate their rights. This was exemplified in the

4. Ibid., p.18.

Falklands and Grenada conflicts, which saw a total collapse of the media's independence as it followed the military diktat in totality.

## Spectacular Media Management in the First Gulf War

Much has been written about the spectacular media management achieved by the US in the First Gulf War. What was remarkable about the American success was that it was used so extensively to spread disinformation and propaganda that its target audience believed everything. The media was excluded from the battlefront except for official briefings and the official clips handed out by the military. The military was highly proactive and provided selected pre-edited and positive news to all branches of the media. As a result, the military was able to control the media image of the conflict. The military not only used the media to present its policies in the best light but also to deceive and misinform the Iraqis. General Schwarzkopf made sure that the media pools were allowed extensive coverage of the Marines' rehearsal of assault. As he expected, this received wide coverage on TV networks and convinced the Iraqis of an invasion from the sea.[5] Disinformation and propaganda were used extensively to propel the military aims successfully.

## Technology in Aid of Media and its Independence

One of the major hampering factors for the mediamen in their war reportage was the unwillingness of the military to accept their presence. The military justified it on the grounds of "operational security" as it rightly felt that the presence of the media and their need to report would lead to the enemy coming to know of its orbat (order of battle) and plans. The second major factor that obstructed the media was having to rely on communication channels provided by the military for onward transmission of its images. Presence of satellites, miniaturisation of photo equipment and advances in communications, presence of global networks, 24 hour news channels, etc have revolutionalised the media's ability to chart an independent course and operate outside the state's and military's control. This was evident in the Kargil conflict wherein the Indian media was well equipped technologically and highly capable of independent reporting. However, in times of war, the "operational security" angle coupled with "social contract" and "patriotism" severely restrict the media's independence. It has given rise to the embedded

5. Ibid., p.166.

journalist, as seen in the recent invasion of Iraq by the US. This clearly permits the military to exploit its immense power for planting disinformation and propaganda. It is even more effective today for, by and large, the media is today perceived to be outside the control of the state. Even though it gets shackled during war, the perception continues to be that of a "free media" providing "factual" coverage. The scheme of "social contract" works subtly and it should be understood by the military that it is in their interest to let the public perceive the media as being "free" of controls. Only then can the disinformation and propaganda planted purposefully produce the desired effect.

## World Wide Web: The Internet

The internet differs from the earliest agents of the media in terms of control. With the traditional mass media, be it the Press, radio or TV, a small group of editors decided which news to print, broadcast or telecast. With the internet, this control has disappeared. The "individual" is the controller. Anyone can create a web page. Bulletin boards and now blogs are used to churn out instant opinions. The ease of internet polling produces results to colour public opinions. Every shade of opinion, on every subject, can be found posted on the world wide web. While it was easier to manipulate the traditional media in war through "social contract," the internet offers a different scenario. As nobody is in charge, who will you manipulate? Nevertheless, the internet, in reality, is a propagandist's delight due to the availability of total freedom and the anonymity offered. The internet accommodates a wide range of views, from radical to moderate, pro-democracy activists to intelligence officers masquerading as anti-establishment rebels. With such a mixed bag, the truth often becomes mangled.[6] Indeed, the internet is the new tool for manipulation. The very opportunities offered by the internet are also its weaknesses.

For disinformation to be effective, it must reach the target audience and it must be credible. The global reach of the internet ensures the first. The second part, of credibility, poses problems. The digital world has unmatched methods of falsifying information, thus, producing doubts on the quality of information. The speed of dissemination, however, works in its favour as humans tend to believe the first image. Therefore, the internet can be exploited profitably for disinformation, specially in combination with other

6. Philip H.J. Davies, "Information Warfare and the Future of the Spy," www.1wrdaphi@reading.ac.uk..

media so that the slur on its veracity does not surface and is instead submerged by its reach and the speed of the reach.

## Media Management in the Internet Age: Kosovo Conflict

The Serbian military reacted to the North Atlantic Treaty Organisation (NATO) bombing of 1999 by dispersing its ground forces throughout the countryside in hard to find locations. Without a ground threat to react to, lack of air superiority and unfavourable weather, NATO bombing failed to destroy much of the Serbian forces, and the conflict dragged on much beyond the few days NATO leaders believed it would take. Milosevic seized this opportunity to portray the Serbs as victims of NATO, and particularly US, aggression. During the conflict, NATO faced a massive Serbian propaganda and disinformation campaign designed to show "collateral damage" in NATO bombing and refugees fleeing due to the air strikes. Possessing low penetration of computers and internet, it mobilised its student population in launching computer attacks and a propaganda campaign on the internet. News reports, photographs and other media rained Serbian propaganda around the world as fast as NATO bombs were raining down upon Serbia. It released gripping pictures of American F-117A and F16C fighters it claimed to have shot down. Pictures of errant bombs that caused civilian destruction and hospitals full of children and the elderly who were victims of NATO bombing were constantly broadcast around the globe to rouse sympathy for Serbia. Through constant and repeated use of the electronic media in near real time, Milosevic left NATO behind, gasping for breath in the propaganda race. So successful was the media blitz by the Serbs that NATO felt compelled to attack the TV stations as TV was perceived as a force multiplier. The point to note here is the asymmetry involved. The NATO forces had the technology behind them but, it was the Serbs who managed to plot, plan and execute a successful propaganda campaign through a combined use of the internet with the traditional media. Admiral Ellis stated in his unpublished after-action report, "The length of war could have been cut in half if the US had made better use of its information warfare unit, the first it had assembled and part of whose task was to present the war in the best light to the media and on the internet."[7]

---

7. Robert D' Amico, Dennis Lyn and Eric Wexler, "Munitions of the Mind," *Strategic Review*, Winter 2001.

The Serbs treated use of propaganda and disinformation not as individual acts but as a coordinated campaign. They used the internet along with other elements of the media in a synchronous manner in near real time. Its effectiveness can be gauged from the fact that it almost succeeded in achieving a near collapse of NATO due to the erosion of popular support amongst its members as the conflict dragged on. The Serbs' reliance on non-lethal weapons of propaganda and disinformation helped them balance the military asymmetry they faced.

## Power of the Image

Two events in India have shown what an image, specially the first image on television, can do. The first was the expose by the Tehelka team. The scandal drew its power from a single image: the shot of Bangaru Laxman greedily scooping up a lakh of rupees in currency notes before stuffing the money into his drawer. That shot, repeated over and over again on every TV channel, finished off the BJP's reputation as a clean party. No amount of explanation could erase the power of the image. The second event was the public outrage caused by the video footage of M. Karunanidhi being manhandled by the Chennai police. The national uproar was almost entirely a consequence of the impact of the television picture. Because the images were so powerful, public opinion turned against Jayalalitha immediately. When the director general of police appeared on TV to defend his force, the anchors treated him with scarcely-veiled contempt. The point to note here is that both the images were provided by interested parties. Tehelka supplied the shots of Laxman's bribe-taking and Sun TV, controlled by DMK members, provided the Karunanidhi footage. Bangaru Laxman claims that the footage was doctored. Similarly, Jayalalitha also says that Sun TV provided selectively-edited visuals, in which the police were made to look bad, while Karunanidhi and Maran gained sympathy. In fact, says Jaya TV, the AIDMK's channel, there is a footage of Maran actively obstructing arrest and even slapping a police officer. But because it was Sun TV's pictures that reached national channels first, that version became accepted as truth. During the Kargil conflict, the then Prime Minister of Pakistan, Mr. Nawaz Sharif, made hectic efforts to garner the support of the international community against the so-called "large scale aggression" by the Indian Armed Forces. He was rebuffed by the Clinton Administration and not even offered the customary lunch which is normally hosted for visiting heads of states. A lasting image telecast repeatedly of the forlorn Nawaz Sharif standing all alone, with his head bowed, while the US officials walked off, sent a powerful message. Nothing could project the hopelessness of Pakistan's position better. It was a big demotivator for Pakistan which capitulated soon thereafter. A powerful image – more importantly, a powerful first image – can have devastating consequence. Timing here is of crucial importance. A powerful visual, whether doctored or unfair, is almost impossible to refute. Here is a major lesson for the military in its quest for using disinformation and propaganda as a weapon of war.

## Campaign Methodology

### Issues

To launch a disinformation or a propaganda campaign, a few issues need to be addressed. What is the larger aim? What do we want the adversary to believe? What are the best tools to achieve it?

### Targets

In all variety of warforms, it is the leaders who define the aims, the methods and the desired conditions of the warform. No state wages war. It is the leaders who do so. The decision to engage in warfare or to terminate it is made by the leaders in the state or the group. Group members or the citizens of the state may influence the leader's decision, but it is primarily the will of the leadership that has to be subdued.

Thus, it is obvious that it is the "mind" of the enemy leadership that has to be manipulated. It would be wrong to presume that there is only "one mind" of the enemy. The enemy is really many individual enemies, many minds. If the enemy is dispersed, separate minds would have to be attacked separately. If the enemy is concentrated, the attack can be centralised. The attacks have to be directed at influencing or manipulating the leader's knowledge or beliefs or indirectly by attacking the knowledge or beliefs of those upon whom the leader depends for action. Leaders and decision-makers are usually not difficult to identify in any organisation hierarchy. Whenever any organisation applies power or force, it assumes hierarchical characteristics. Thus, the knowledge and beliefs of the decision-makers are

8. Colonel Richard Szafranski, USAF, "A Theory of Information Warfare – Preparing for 2020," *Aerospace Chronicles*, Spring 1995.

the Achilles heel of hierarchies.[8] The aim of any campaign involving disinformation and propaganda should be to affect the adversary decision-makers in such a way that the decisions result in actions that support our military aims.

**Affecting Beliefs**

India, as a democratic country with a free Press, is slowly developing an identity of independent opinion amongst the news analysts. Compared with a closed society like China, which has a highly secretive and politically controlled media, information obtained from independent sources like BBC, CNN and the Indian media will appear to be more authentic and true. Such a "belief" can be utilised advantageously to propagate the notion that whatever "closed door systems" like China offer is untrue. At a critical time, such discredit can change the quality of the "fog of war". To cite an example would probably serve as a forceful illustration. Today's technology and computer simulation makes everything possible. In the movie "Forest Gump" the hero is shown shaking hands with John Fitzgerald Kennedy who died almost four decades ago. "Titanic" and "Matrix" are good examples of the power of the computers to create "reality", that is more believable. It will, thus, be possible to use available clips of the leader of the opposing nation, and doctor these to show as if he is rejecting peaceful negotiations. These doctored clips, telecast at the appropriate moment, can be used to camouflage or justify an offensive action by the military. Nobody will believe the subsequent denials as everyone would have "seen" the clips. The video clips of the arrest of Karunanidhi telecast repeatedly had such an impact that all subsequent denials failed to erase the sympathy the DMK leader had obtained.

**Organisation**

Such campaigns are policy decisions that have to work top downwards. A very careful analysis needs to be made of the strategic aim which then has to be broken down to its tactical parts. Continuous monitoring and feedback of the success or otherwise are extremely crucial elements of such a campaign. Another very important aspect is the timing. The timing for execution has to be selected very carefully, specially if the vehicle for execution of the campaign happens to be the media. What is obvious is that a dedicated organisation needs to be created that can organise and harmonise the various elements so that the results are in tune with one's aims. It must have a "think-tank" cell which can translate the strategic aim into tangible tactical goals. Pre-planned presentations mixing fact with inference to influence decisions will have to be prepared. Studies show that individuals give weightage to information in the order in which it is received. Such bias and other psychological weaknesses will have to be exploited.

## Who will be the Members of this Think-Tank?

Apart from the Services and the Ministries of Defence and External Affairs, all the other decision-makers of our national security apparatus must be represented. It must possess the technical back-up and computer specialists who can doctor or manipulate the visuals – be they film/television clips or mere photographs. The available intelligence and operations elements in Headquarters Integrated Defence Staff could be utilised for forming such a cell which could then be tasked for scenario building and contingency planning. As time is of crucial importance, this cell must have a direct link-up with the top-most decision-makers so that its expertise can be drawn upon instantaneously. Only then, would we be able to use the weapon of disinformation effectively.

### Advance Planning

In this age of media proliferation, one good example to follow would be of the ad campaign market research groups who carry out surveys to find out the likes and dislikes of their customer target groups in terms of media preferences.

If the enemy's leadership has a preference for CNN, BBC or Al Jazeera, then that should be the vehicle for the onslaught. The internet has a special advantage in that it also enables "customised propaganda." Information can specially be tailored to suit the target audience's weakness. All such efforts will have to be on long-term basis and, hence, the need for a specialist organisation. While dealing with the media, timing is of critical essence. These campaigns will have to be prepared well in advance for various contingencies. The speed of the media and the needs of the media all relate to crucial timing and only pre-planned campaigns with a possibility of last minute modification promise effectiveness.

### Indian Expertise

Can the existing military-media organisation handle such campaigns?

Currently, the Directorate of Public Relations (Defence) which is an element in the Ministry of Defence, handles the media on matters of defence. It has representation from the three Services but is predominantly a bureaucrat controlled organisation with little specialist calibre or understanding of matters military or media. It is designed to handle peace-time interaction. During the Kargil conflict, a Press briefing by combined representatives of the Ministry of External Affairs and the two involved Services was institutionalised on a temporary basis. Both the Army and the Air Force created an ad hoc element to handle the media. There is nothing to suggest that the Army and the Air Force attempted disinformation and propaganda during the Kargil conflict even though Barkha Dutt of Star News was at the "front" with the troops. (A precursor of the "embedded journalist" of the Iraq invasion by the US.) It is time the respective defence planners sat down and created an organisation so that in the future these two non-lethal weapons of war viz. disinformation and propaganda, are utilised effectively to further one's military aim. What is suggested are small specialised cells. They should have both horizontal and vertical connectivity between various Ministries/Services/elements. That disinformation should find a place in the planning and execution of military operations at the tactical level needs no emphasis. In fact, most military campaigns and operations include such aspects. What is needed is an awareness that in the new millennium, information plays a very crucial role and is extremely vulnerable to manipulation. It is this vulnerability that must be exploited.

## Conclusion

Towards the end of the twentieth century, the search began for weapons that minimise destruction by offering precision, with no collateral damage and, eventually, weapons that don't kill – non-lethal weapons. In this vast non-lethal armoury that is being developed, two of the oldest non-lethal weapons are already available – disinformation and propaganda. Both have been used extensively in the past successfully. The marvels of technology that have led to the information age have again brought these two weapons into prominence as today information is power and these two weapons directly affect the very perception of information – by manipulating it.

The vehicles of propelling these two non-lethal weapons are the myriad forms of the media that have evolved. The media has a prominent place in society as it is in the very heart of today's civilisation, referred to as the information or the knowledge age. The media's role is to keep the citizen informed. It is perceived to be a "free agent", uncontrolled by the state. However, as has been seen, but for a few exceptions, it is managed by the state and the military in times of war to aid and further the military's aim. The perception that the media continues to be "free" during war lingers on even after peace has been interrupted by war. It is to the military's advantage that such a perception persists for it enables the military to manipulate the information flow through its disinformation and propaganda campaigns.

Multiplicity of media, the internet, the convergence of media technologies all point to a future where the "control" on the information will slowly slip, and the individual and his ability to manipulate the information will triumph. Veracity or truth will be at a premium. Anonymity is one of the chief attributes of the world wide web. It is an ideal ground for a propagandist, with ample scope for manipulation, spoilt by the premium on veracity. Unless the disinformation or the propaganda is believed, it is useless as a weapon. Kosovo has shown that a way out exists. The weakness of the human psyche being to believe the first "arrived" message, the speed of the internet, and its vast global footprint are some of the factors that favour the propagandist. The power of the image, specially the first image, has a phenomenal opportunity for the military to exploit when it uses these two non-lethal weapons. These weapons don't cost much. For very little, they deliver an effect worth crores.

It is time the military seizes this opportunity with both hands. But the military alone cannot produce the desired result. All the elements that are responsible for national security must get into the act. For disinformation and propaganda campaigns to be successful, a dedicated organisation is needed to be carved that has the necessary technical back-up, is able to coordinate and interact horizontally and vertically, and has the total support from the top of the hierarchy. It is time the defence planners and others responsible for national security address these issues so that both disinformation and propaganda are utilised effectively to enhance national security. ❑

# Indigenisation Vs Import: Indian Defence Industry

(Extracts from an address at ASSOCHAM)

With a sustained economic growth of over 8 per cent in the past four years, foreign exchange reserves of over $ 288 billion, a market of over a billion people and a modernising armed force of over a million, India is a country that is sending ripples across the globe as she creates a niche for herself in the realm of global influence. A country with enormous potential, immense capability, resilient foundations and a rich heritage, India is set to play an important role in the international arena of geo-politics. It is against this backdrop that I consider it a privilege indeed to share my views on the theme of this significant seminar on “Indigenisation Versus Import: Indian Defence Industry.” I thank the organisers for giving me this opportunity to present my views to such an experienced and enriched international august gathering.

The post-independence vision for the Indian defence industry resulted in the creation of a model that hinged on the Defence Research and Development Organisation (DRDO) for R&D and the Public Sector Undertakings (PSUs) and Ordnance Factories to deliver the goods. It was a very simplistic model with a limited budget. In its nascent years, the defence industry, being designated as a core sector, was exclusively controlled by the central government. Bureaucratic control, with little accountability and minimal peripheral participation by the private sector, created an environment which remained tightly controlled and non-competitive. Scarce resources, unending timelines, “blame game” with the Armed Forces and the reluctance of advanced countries to share high-end technology further compounded the problem. The end result was that India was forced to seek a solution through imports to meet the requirements of defence. Whatever limited indigenisation efforts were made, remained restricted to the post-import scenario. In spite of these shortcomings, there were some noteworthy indigenous successes through this model like the LCA, the ALH, modern warships and the guided missile programmes.

With globalisation and liberalisation of the Indian economy, the GDP and overall growth rates began to edge higher as did the successive defence budgets. Our leaders also realised that to transform the nation into a global player, the country could not afford to depend continuously on imports for its defence needs It was evident that the existing model of our defence industry was not giving the desired result. All this set in motion the process of progressive change in policies. In 2001, the government decided to open up the defence industry for private sector participation up to 100 per cent by allowing 26 per cent foreign direct investment (FDI). Unfortunately, this did not succeed as the private sector was wary of investing huge capital that is needed in the defence production due to the apprehensions of not having assured supply orders. As a result, in 2004, the Kelkar Committee was constituted to review the methodologies adopted by our public sector dedicated to defence and produce a framework that would encourage the entry of the private sector into defence. It is rather unfortunate that progress on the recommendations of this committee is rather slow.

I too was perplexed at the lack of involvement of the private sector in the defence industry. I assessed that one of the reasons could be that the industry was not aware of the true requirements of the Armed Forces. Hence, in 2005, during my tenure as assistant chief at HQ IDS, I produced a document titled "Technology Needs of the Armed Forces." Through the Confederation of Indian Industry (CII), I had made it available to CII members. In order to generate an exchange of ideas and interest in the subject, I had also organised interactive sessions with private industry players. Most of the members who attended these sessions opined that the private sector was chary of participating due to the complexities involved in procedural issues and the uneconomical model of the industry in which volumes involved were low. Obviously, there was much more to be done to coax the private sector to involve itself in the defence industry.

With a hefty defence budget for fiscal 2007-08 of Rs. 96,000 crore that includes a capital budget of Rs. 42,000 crore and nearly US$ 30 billion of imports planned over the next four years, the amounts involved are astronomical. This has created an opportunity for us to tap this potential towards boosting indigenous capability. This opportunity was translated by the Ministry of Defence (MoD) into the "Offset Policy". Realising that the private sector was keen on participating in the defence industry and needed inputs in the form of advanced technology and some finance, the MoD put forth the Offset Policy which ruled that whenever large imports were involved, it would be mandatory for the exporting firm to invest a percentage of the total amount into the Indian defence industry. It was assessed that this would, in the long-term, build up our indigenous technological capability in defence production. This, indeed, is an excellent opportunity for our defence industry to take giant strides towards building our very own defence equipments.

I am impressed by the achievement of the Indian group Mahindra and Mahindra in being able to not only produce but also market military vehicles to a country like Israel, one of the biggest sellers of defence equipment to India. At the same time, I fail to understand why our country cannot reap the benefits of such indigenous capability. What stops us then from tapping such domestic potential? I think that it is time we do "out of the box" thinking. We need to follow the "Merger and Acquisition" route. Take a look at the way the steel giant Mittal Group operates. The group buys steel factories that are not performing efficiently, pumps in capital, infuses newer management techniques and churns the stagnant factory into a world-class one. Can we apply this methodology selectively to our present defence industry too? What I am suggesting is strategic acquisition. Suppose we identify a major player like the Tatas or Ambanis or the Mahindras. Offer a strategic sale of a DRDO lab and a PSU that matches their interest in defence equipment. Such a strategic marriage would produce a "win-win" situation for all. The private player will acquire a readymade R&D facility complete with its scientists and a manufacturing hub that already is involved in defence production. All that the player needs to do is provide the expert management, infuse some technology and capital into the scheme, use its superior marketing skills, and we have the successful Mittal Formula replicated.

Our space scientists also offer us a good lesson. The model followed for procurement by the Indian Space Research Organisation (ISRO) is to involve a private firm as a co-partner in developing a project or equipment. Once the equipment is ready for production, the co-partner is given the contract for production. This model does not resort to "lowest bidder" procedures that are applicable in the defence sector. The model also gives ISRO the flexibility to choose the private sector as co-partners. Ironically, both, the MoD and ISRO are governmental organisations following vastly different procurement methodologies. Surely we can derive learning values from the success of ISRO and apply these to defence deals.

In our Department of Defence Production, bureaucrats looking after various PSUs function under the Raksha Mantri. However, there is no bureaucrat who is responsible for the private industry. We definitely need officials in the government who will perform the role of "enablers" to modify the procedures and facilitate the active participation of the private sector in defence production.

The route towards indigenisation has been a long and eventful one. Despite the decades, India has not been able to achieve the vision that was set out for her defence industry. With a rising economy, a growing industrial base and Armed Forces acclaimed the world over, India cannot be reliant on imports to meet her defence needs. It is time that India becomes truly self-sufficient in this sector. We are at the crossroads of a historic juncture which offers us the opportunity to make a significant change. There is no doubt that the Armed Forces must be at the cutting edge at all times. That is possible only if the Armed Forces have the best equipment. Today, the best cutting edge technology, unfortunately, is only available outside the country. Therefore, we need to create an environment that elevates the defence industry to the level where it is able to provide indigenous equipment to our Armed Forces. I think that the right moment for such an elevation of our defence industry has arrived and we must not let this moment slip away. ❑

# Jointness: The British Model

I had the opportunity to go through the previous three issues of "The Purple Pages" recently. It was very heartening to get a first hand glimpse of what the middle-level leadership desires. Page after page is devoted to "how to be joint." While we must carve out our unique Indian method of being joint, it may help us to know how others have done it. In September 2005, I was fortunate to visit the Permanent Joint Headquarters (PJHQ) in London. PJHQ is headed by Chief of Joint Operations (CJO). At that time, the CJO was Air Marshal Sir Glenn Tropy KCB, DSO, CDE. He briefed us on the mission and role of the PJHQ. The salient features are given below.

## Background

After the Falklands War and the involvement in Gulf War I, and the Bosnia and Kosvo experience, it was realised that single Service operations were very expensive and had serious shortcoming. A Defence Costs Study (DCS) was undertaken in 1994. It brought out that handling of defence by a single Service in the UK was ad hoc, reactive, duplicative, expensive and not truly joint. Therefore, it recommended formation of a Joint Headquarters which would enhance operational efficiency and effectiveness as well as achieve financial savings. This was expectedly opposed by the defence community but the Secretary of State accepted the proposal. The division of responsibility broadly was to keep the handling of strategic policy with the Ministry of Defence (MoD), hand over conduct of operations to Joint Headquarters and let the single Services support and deliver the required military capability.

With this background, Permanent Joint Headquarters was established on 1 April 1996, at Northwood, London, in the UK.

## Mission and Role of PJHQ

The mission and role of PJHQ are:

- Provide politically aware military advice to the MoD.
- Exercise operational command of the UK forces assigned to overseas joint and combined operations.
- In conjunction with the Services and MoD, develop the UK's joint war-fighting capabilities.

### Additional Tasks

In addition to the primary tasks as listed above, the following additional tasks have been allotted:-

- Monitor designated areas of operational interest.
- Contingency planning.
- Exercise OPCOM of overseas Commands.
- Formulate JW doctrine at Op/Tac levels.
- Conduct joint force exercises.
- Focus for joint rapid reaction force planning and exercising.
- Advise/assess joint capabilities/standards.

### Operational Control

It controls the UK forces operationally in Iraq, Bosnia, Kosovo and Afghanistan. Six deployments in Bahrain, Diego Garcia, Cyprus, etc and 5 UN peace-keeping missions are also under its control.

### Areas Excluded from PJHQ

The areas excluded from the ambit of PJHQ are:-

- Strategic nuclear deterrent.
- Defence of UK home base.
- Territorial Ireland.
- Northern Ireland.
- Counter-terrorism in UK.
- NATO Article V (General War).

### PJHQ Organisaion

PJHQ is staffed with personnel from the three Services and civilians. The manning ratio is 33 per cent from the Army, 28 per cent from the Air Force, 25 per cent from the Navy and 14 per cent civilians.

PJHQ is headed by the Chief of Joint Operation (CJO). He has two deputies – DCJO (Ops) and CJO (Op Support) and a civilian Command

Secretary who provides policy, legal and financial advice.

PJHQ has 11 divisions. The specific responsibility of each division is:-

| | | |
|---|---|---|
| J1 | – | Personnel |
| J2 | – | Operational Int |
| J3 | – | Current Ops |
| J4 | – | Logistic/Medical |
| J5 | – | Crisis and Deliberate Planning |
| J6 | – | Communication and Information Systems |
| J7 | – | Joint Training |
| J8 | – | Finance and Human Resources |
| J9 | – | Policy, Legal, Presentation |
| JFHQ | – | Deployable Headquarter |
| JF Log C HQ | – | Deployable Logistic Component HQ |

## Single Service Commands and Joint Rapid Reaction Force (JRRF)

The C-in-C of the Single Service Commands deliver fully manned, trained and equipped force elements (ships, tanks, aircraft, for example) at readiness for operations. These forces are made available through the Joint Rapid Reaction Force. Single Services provide Component HQs which when committed to an operation, work as part of the in-theatre force, under the direction of the Joint Task Force HQ (JTFHQ). To command the JRRF, a fully resourced JTFHQ is maintained at 48 hrs notice to move. Along with JTFHQ, a Joint Force Logistic Component HQ is also maintained.

## Higher Defence Organisation Meetings

The Secretary of State, CDS, C-in-C of Single Services and the CJO meet weekly to ensure that they all are working unitarily without differences.

## Conclusion

Financial wastages and lack of jointness in matters military forced the civilian defence leadership in the UK to adopt a new military model in which a permanent Joint HQ was created. Command of all operations outside the UK was entrusted to it. Single Services were left with the task of providing trained and ready components to this Joint Command. Rapid reaction is the keyword of operational readiness. In its evolution, PJHQ has also been given additional tasks involving long-term contingency planning, creation of joint doctrines, intelligence monitoring of areas of operational interest and advising/assessing joint capabilities.

## A Macro Comparison with our Model of Jointness

Like in India and other countries, it was leadership other than the military which foisted a "joint" model on the British forces. The basic rationale which propelled such an action was wasteful expenditure and a desire to increase operational efficiency. Recognition of similar lacunae led to the creation of Integrated Defence Staff (IDS) in India. A large number of elements that are present in PJHQ are also present in IDS. The major difference lies in operational control. IDS possesses none. While the PP&FD branch of HQ IDS is doing a sterling job in ensuring commonality, interoperability and a more efficient procurement cycle of new equipment, the other aspect of increasing operational efficiency through jointness is yet to be addressed. ❑